P9-DMS-666

The Diary of
Anne Frank

The Diary of Anne Frank

A Play in Two Acts

Dramatized by

FRANCES GOODRICH and ALBERT HACKETT

Based upon the book

ANNE FRANK: THE DIARY OF A YOUNG GIRL

with a Foreword by

BROOKS ATKINSON

Notes and Questions by

N. D. MacDONALD, M.A., B.ED.   J. I. DOWNIE, B.A.

IRWIN PUBLISHING

Toronto, Canada

Copyright, as an unpublished work, 1954, by Albert Hackett, Frances Goodrich Hackett and Otto Frank

Copyright, as an unpublished work, 1956, by Albert Hackett and Frances Goodrich Hackett

© Copyright, 1956, by Albert Hackett, Frances Goodrich Hackett and Otto Frank

© Copyright, 1958, by Albert Hackett, Frances Goodrich Hackett and Otto Frank (Acting Edition)

© Irwin Publishing , 1964
A Former Book Society of Canada Limited Book

ISBN 0 7725-5060-3

Thanks is due to Fred Fell, New York, for permission to reproduce, for the cover and text, halftones from the Broadway production.

The present text of *The Diary of Anne Frank* is intended primarily for reading and study in the secondary schools of Canada. It may be privately read and studied. This edition may not be used for public use by amateur producing groups. The Dramatists Play Service, Inc., 14 East 38th Street, New York, N.Y. 10016 is the exclusive publisher of the amateur acting edition. Any group wishing to present an amateur production of the play should write directly to the Dramatists Play Service, which will supply acting editions for production purposes. A royalty is payable to the Dramatists Play Service in advance of production. Upon payment of such royalty formal authorization for the production will be furnished by the Play Service.

Inquiries on stock rights in the United States and Canada should be addressed to Samuel French, 25 West 45th Street, New York 36, N.Y.

No performance of any other kind may be given without permission in writing from the authors' agent, Leah Salisbury, Inc., 234 West 44th Street, New York 36, N.Y.

The copying, either of separate parts or the whole, of this work by any process whatsoever is forbidden by law and subject to the penalties prescribed in the Copyright Act.

12 13 14 15   WC   94 93 92 91

FOREWORD

When the annual rite of prize-giving occurred in the spring of 1956, *The Diary of Anne Frank* took all the honours. First, the Antoinette Perry Award; second, the Critics' Circle Award; third, the Pulitzer Prize, to list them chronologically.

They brought the highest honour of the season to Frances Goodrich and Albert Hackett (Mr. and Mrs. Hackett), who wrote the dramatization, and to everyone associated with the lovely stage production in New York. Behind the theatre artists stood the shining image of a little Jewish girl who, at the age of fifteen, died in the Nazi concentration camp at Bergen-Belsen in March, 1945. The prizes and public veneration for the play were a tribute to the spirit of an adolescent girl.

If Anne Frank, author of the original diary, had survived the barbarism of the Nazis, she would have been twenty-seven years of age. She was an alert and high-spirited girl who hoped to be a writer. How jubilant and proud she would have been if she could have been in New York during the prize-giving season! It would have confirmed the ambitions she confided to her diary during the two years when she was fighting boredom, bickering and misery in an attic in Amsterdam. Everything that one says about the play, one says about Anne Frank. For the triumph of the play lies in the delicacy with which it preserves the bloom of her adolescence and the grace of her spirit.

The play dramatizes *Anne Frank: The Diary of a Young Girl*, published in an English translation in America in 1952. Anne was the youngest of a group of eight Jews who for two years and one month hid in a cramped attic over a warehouse to escape the Gestapo. The Gestapo was then engaged in the grisly operation of shipping Jews to concentration camps as meat packers ship livestock to slaughter. In addition to Anne, the eight included her father, mother and sister, another couple and their son, who was three years older than Anne, and a middle-aged dentist, who joined them later when it

v

was clear that the Gestapo was getting around to him. We are told that thousands of Jews were in hiding in other places. But we have a vivid knowledge of the eight Jews confined in an attic because Anne gaily continued to keep the diary she had begun on her thirteenth birthday, when she was still attending school with no foreknowledge of the ordeal in store for her family.

Thanks to the diary we know the homely details of this almost incredible example of the will to survive and of the selflessness of a few friends on the outside who provided food and protection. For more than two years, eight human beings never went outdoors, kept completely silent for about ten hours every day when strangers were working in the warehouse downstairs, never stood by a window during daylight, never discarded rubbish that might betray them, never drew water or flushed the toilet when there was anyone else in the building, never did anything that might indicate that the attic was anything except an abandoned storehouse.

If eight people of different ages from different families had succeeded in maintaining such a sensational secret for a week, it would have seemed remarkable. But to have kept the secret for two years and a month would seem fantastic if the diary and other records did not exist to prove it.

The diary would not have such a deep hold on the affections of the world if it were merely a record of events and techniques. Fundamentally, it is a portrait of adolescence. The privations and the emotional strains of the secret household are hardly more than background. In the foreground is the figure of an enchanting girl. Her vitality rushes at the reader. Anne's inner life flourishes. She had every reason to look forward to the career of a writer. For her diary is an extraordinary mirror of a human being on the threshold of life —temperamental, impulsive, brash, but also intelligent, thoughtful, affectionate and aspiring.

Things that are irritating and things that are winning are tightly interwoven. Although she is frequently too restless for the comfort of an anxious household, she is also studious and religious, aware of the mysteries of life and eager to penetrate them. "Little bundle of contradictions" she calls herself in the last item in her diary before the frightful day when the police raided the attic and carried everyone off to concentration camp.

Like an alert adolescent, she has some mature ideas rattling around in her busy head. She has enough skill as a writer to express ideas easily. Her photograph shows a beautiful maiden with an oval face, black hair in a jaunty bob, lively eyes and a sweet mouth. None of the documents or statistics related to the abominations of the Nazis is so accusing as this diary. It reminds us that the Nazis murdered not only lives but life. They murdered a radiant part of the future.

Strange how the spirit of an immature, obscure girl in Amsterdam during the war has crossed the Atlantic and tested the skill and sensitivity of a group of adult theatre people! The professionals found themselves under a heavy obligation to represent her truthfully. Since diaries are diffuse and chaotic, they set playwrights some difficult problems. For plays do need themes and form. Every word in a good play has to be pertinent.

Mr. and Mrs. Hackett wrote eight drafts of *The Diary of Anne Frank* before they felt that they had represented Anne fairly. Although they have quoted lines from the diary, the play is virtually an independent work. The diary is subjective. But Mr. and Mrs. Hackett have had to create a play that takes an objective point of view toward a group of people of whom Anne is only one, and not necessarily the pivotal one. In the organization and management of the household, Anne's father is the decisive character. Mr. and Mrs. Hackett have had to find concrete devices for explaining traits of character that are only described in the diary. They have had to concentrate intangible movement in specific dramatic acts. They have had to put the diary in perspective against the events of history that occurred after the police raided the attic in 1944. Most of all, they have had to provide a beginning, middle and end.

The reader of the diary is hardly aware of what they have done, the craftsmanship and writing are so unobtrusive. The play is neither heroic nor sentimental. Written in a subdued key, without pointing a moral, it chronicles the plain details of a strange adventure, some of it distressing, some of it humorous, but all of it warm, simple and affecting.

Although Mr. and Mrs. Hackett have contributed craftsmanship, they have not lost the glow of Anne's character.
Their key sentence comes from one of Anne's last observa-
tions in her diary: "In spite of everything, I still believe that
people are really good at heart." Everything in the play
bears on that point—the quarrels, the intrigue and the terror
bearing out the truth of the first phrase in the sentence; the
loyalty, the forgiveness and the kindness bearing out the
truth of the sentence proper. Although Anne was a born
writer, it would have been a miracle if, at the age of twenty-
seven, she could herself have told this story in the theatre
as tenderly and truthfully as Mr. and Mrs. Hackett have in
their play.

By the time any play reaches the stage, it has become a
group enterprise. What the playwrights put on paper reaches
the audience through the minds and gifts of the actors, director, scene designer and producer. Once Kermit Bloomgarden
had persuaded Mr. and Mrs. Hackett to write the play, *The
Diary of Anne Frank* became virtually a mission. Everyone
approached the production with a particular sense of respon-
sibility. Garson Kanin, who had undertaken to direct the
performance, went to Amsterdam to meet Anne's father, who
came from Switzerland to help. Although Mr. and Mrs.
Hackett had completed the script, they went, too. For ten
days Mr. Kanin and Mr. and Mrs. Hackett visited the attic,
studied the neighbourhood, listened to the street and canal
sounds and ransacked Mr. Frank's mind and memory for
details and general impressions.

By the time Mr. Kanin called the actors together, he was
able to provide them with a point of view and a mood. Since
the warehouse is narrow, the actual living quarters of the
refugees in the play were on a perpendicular scale. In his
stage design, Boris Aronson translated the same environ-
ment into the horizontal dimensions of the stage, portraying
the cramped, shabby interior, and suggesting also the outdoors of a city tense from the presence of the Nazis.

Combining instinct for the theatre with precise knowledge
of the theme, Mr. Kanin was able to cast the play flawlessly.
When it opened in the autumn of 1955, the performance was
especially notable for two of the actors who were in it. Jo-

seph Schildkraut, who played the part of Anne's father, gave the performance a solid underpinning by his quiet command of the whole situation and his restrained gentleness. In her first Broadway part, Susan Strasberg, seventeen years of age, played Anne with mercurial spontaneity and purity of soul that gave the performance exaltation and beauty. Like the work as a whole, her performance was overflowing with life but never self-conscious. The play deserved this sort of acting.

Through every line of it shines the spirit of Anne Frank. For the most part, it is a smiling spirit. By preserving it so delicately, Mr. and Mrs. Hackett have let a clean, young mind address the conscience of the world.

BROOKS ATKINSON

THE DIARY OF ANNE FRANK *was first presented by Kermit Bloomgarden at the Cort Theatre, New York City, on October 5, 1955, with the following cast:*

(IN ORDER OF APPEARANCE)

MR. FRANK	Joseph Schildkraut
MIEP	Gloria Jones
MRS. VAN DAAN	Dennie Moore
MR. VAN DAAN.	Lou Jacobi
PETER VAN DAAN	David Levin
MRS. FRANK	Gusti Huber
MARGOT FRANK	Eva Rubinstein
ANNE FRANK	Susan Strasberg
MR. KRALER	Clinton Sundberg
MR. DUSSEL	Jack Gilford

Directed by Garson Kanin

Production designed by Boris Aronson

Costumes by Helene Pons

Lighting by Leland Watson

The guidance of Mr. Otto H. Frank, Dr. L. de Jong, Miss Lidia Winkle and The Netherlands State Institute for War Documentation, Amsterdam, is gratefully acknowledged.

The Time: During the years of World War II and immediately thereafter.

The Place: Amsterdam

There are two acts

ACT ONE

Scene 1

The scene remains the same throughout the play. It is the top floor of a warehouse and office building in Amsterdam, Holland. The sharply peaked roof of the building is outlined against a sea of other rooftops, stretching away into the distance. Nearby is the belfry of a church tower, the Westertoren, whose carillon rings out the hours. Occasionally faint sounds float up from below: the voices of children playing in the street, the tramp of marching feet, a boat whistle from the canal.

The three rooms of the top floor and a small attic space above are exposed to our view. The largest of the rooms is in the centre, with two small rooms, slightly raised, on either side. On the right is a bathroom, out of sight. A narrow steep flight of stairs at the back leads up to the attic. The rooms are sparsely furnished with a few chairs, cots, a table or two. The windows are painted over, or covered with makeshift blackout curtains. In the main room there is a sink, a gas ring for cooking and a wood-burning stove for warmth.

The room on the left is hardly more than a closet. There is a skylight in the sloping ceiling. Directly under this room is a small steep stairwell, with steps leading down to a door. This is the only entrance from the building below. When the door is opened we see that it has been concealed on the outer side by a bookcase attached to it.

The curtain rises on an empty stage. It is late afternoon November, 1945.

The rooms are dusty, the curtains in rags. Chairs and tables are overturned.

The door at the foot of the small stairwell swings open. Mr. Frank comes up the steps into view. He is a gentle, cultured European in his middle years. There is still a trace of a German accent in his speech.

He stands looking slowly around, making a supreme effort at self-control. He is weak, ill. His clothes are threadbare.

1

After a second he drops his rucksack on the couch and moves slowly about. He opens the door to one of the smaller rooms, and then abruptly closes it again, turning away. He goes to the window at the back, looking off at the Westertoren as its carillon strikes the hour of six, then he moves restlessly on.

From the street below we hear the sound of a barrel organ and children's voices at play. There is a many-coloured scarf hanging from a nail. Mr. Frank takes it, putting it around his neck. As he starts back for his rucksack, his eye is caught by something lying on the floor. It is a woman's white glove. He holds it in his hand and suddenly all of his self-control is gone. He breaks down, crying.

We hear footsteps on the stairs. Miep Gies comes up, looking for Mr. Frank. Miep is a Dutch girl of about twenty-two. She wears a coat and hat, ready to go home. She is pregnant. Her attitude toward Mr. Frank is protective, compassionate.

MIEP.   Are you all right ,Mr. Frank?

MR. FRANK, *quickly controlling himself.*   Yes, Miep, yes.

MIEP.   Everyone in the office has gone home . . . It's after six. *Then pleading.* Don't stay up here, Mr. Frank. What's the use of torturing yourself like this?

MR. FRANK.   I've come to say good-bye . . . I'm leaving here, Miep.

MIEP.   What do you mean? Where are you going? Where?

MR. FRANK.   I don't know yet. I haven't decided.

MIEP.   Mr. Frank, you can't leave here! This is your home! Amsterdam is your home. Your business is here, waiting for you . . . You're needed here . . . Now that the war is over, there are things that . . .

MR. FRANK.   I can't stay in Amsterdam, Miep. It has too many memories for me. Everywhere there's something . . . the house we lived in . . . the school . . . that street organ playing out there . . . I'm not the person you used to know, Miep. I'm a bitter old man. *Breaking off.* Forgive me. I shouldn't speak to you like this . . . after all that you did for us . . . the suffering . . .

MIEP.   No. No. It wasn't suffering. You can't say we suffered.

As she speaks, she straightens a chair which is overturned.

MR. FRANK.   I know what you went through, you and Mr.
Kraler. I'll remember it as long as I live. *He gives one last look
around.* Come, Miep. *He starts for the steps, then remembers
his rucksack, going back to get it.*
MIEP, *hurrying up to a cupboard.*   Mr. Frank, did you see?
There are some of your papers here. *She brings a bundle of
papers to him.* We found them in a heap of rubbish on the
floor after . . . after you left.
MR. FRANK.   Burn them. *He opens his rucksack to put the
glove in it.*
MIEP.   But, Mr. Frank, there are letters, notes . . .
MR. FRANK.   Burn them. All of them.
MIEP.   Burn *this? She hands him a paperbound notebook.*
MR. FRANK, *quietly.*   Anne's diary. *He opens the diary and
begins to read.* "Monday, the sixth of July, nineteen forty-two."
To Miep. Nineteen forty-two. Is it possible, Miep? . . . Only
three years ago. *As he continues his reading, he sits down on
the couch.* "Dear Diary, since you and I are going to be great
friends, I will start by telling you about myself. My name is
Anne Frank. I am thirteen years old. I was born in Germany
the twelfth of June, nineteen twenty-nine. As my family is
Jewish, we emigrated to Holland when Hitler came to power."
*As Mr. Frank reads on, another voice joins his, as if coming
from the air. It is Anne's voice.*
MR. FRANK AND ANNE.   "My father started a business, import-
ing spice and herbs. Things went well for us until nineteen
forty. Then the war came, and the Dutch capitulation, followed
by the arrival of the Germans. Then things got very bad for the
Jews." *Mr. Frank's voice dies out. Anne's voice continues
alone. The lights dim slowly to darkness. The curtain falls on
the scene.*
ANNE'S VOICE.   You could not do this and you could not do
that. They forced Father out of his business. We had to wear
yellow stars. I had to turn in my bike. I couldn't go to a Dutch
school any more. I couldn't go to the movies, or ride in an automobile, or even on a street-car, and a million other things. But
somehow we children still managed to have fun. Yesterday
Father told me we were going into hiding. Where, he wouldn't
say. At five o'clock this morning Mother woke me and told me

to hurry and get dressed. I was to put on as many clothes as I could. It would look too suspicious if we walked along carrying suitcases. It wasn't until we were on our way that I learned where we were going. Our hiding place was to be upstairs in the building where Father used to have his business. Three other people were coming in with us . . . the van Daans and their son Peter . . . Father knew the van Daans but we had never met them . . . *During the last lines the curtain rises on the scene. The lights dim on. Anne's voice fades out.*

Scene 2

It is early morning, July, 1942. The rooms are bare, as before, but they are now clean and orderly.

Mr. van Daan, a tall, portly man in his late forties, is in the main room, pacing up and down, nervously smoking a cigarette. His clothes and overcoat are expensive and well cut.

Mrs. van Daan sits on the couch, clutching her possessions, a hatbox, bags, etc. She is a pretty woman in her early forties. She wears a fur coat over her other clothes.

Peter van Daan is standing at the window of the room on the right, looking down at the street below. He is a shy, awkward boy of sixteen. He wears a cap, a raincoat, and long Dutch trousers, like "plus fours." At his feet is a black case, a carrier for his cat.

The yellow Star of David is conspicuous on all of their clothes.

MRS. VAN DAAN, *rising, nervous, excited.*   Something's happened to them! I know it!

MR. VAN DAAN.   Now, Kerli!

MRS. VAN DAAN.   Mr. Frank said they'd be here at seven o'clock. He said . . .

MR. VAN DAAN.   They have two miles to walk. You can't expect . . .

MRS. VAN DAAN.   They've been picked up. That's what's happened. They've been taken . . . *Mr. van Daan indicates that he hears someone coming.*

MR. VAN DAAN.   You see? *Peter takes up his carrier and his schoolbag, etc., and goes into the main room as Mr. Frank comes up the stairwell from below. Mr. Frank looks much younger now. His movements are brisk, his manner confident. He wears an overcoat and carries his hat and a small cardboard box. He crosses to the van Daans, shaking hands with each of them.*

MR. FRANK. Mrs. van Daan, Mr. van Daan, Peter. *Then, in explanation of their lateness.* There were too many of the Green Police on the streets . . . we had to take the long way around. *Up the steps come Margot Frank, Mrs. Frank, Miep (not pregnant now) and Mr. Kraler. All of them carry bags, packages, and so forth. The Star of David is conspicuous on all of the Franks' clothing. Margot is eighteen, beautiful, quiet, shy. Mrs. Frank is a young mother, gently bred, reserved. She, like Mr. Frank, has a slight German accent. Mr. Kraler is a Dutchman, dependable, kindly.*

As Mr. Kraler and Miep go upstage to put down their parcels, Mrs. Frank turns back to call Anne.

MRS. FRANK. Anne? *Anne comes running up the stairs. She is thirteen, quick in her movements, interested in everything, mercurial in her emotions. She wears a cape, long wool socks and carries a schoolbag.*

MR. FRANK, *introducing them.* My wife, Edith. Mr. and Mrs. van Daan. *Mrs. Frank hurries over, shaking hands with them . . . their son, Peter . . . my daughters, Margot and Anne. Anne gives a polite little curtsy as she shakes Mr. van Daan's hand. Then she immediately starts off on a tour of investigation of her new home, going upstairs to the attic room. Miep and Mr. Kraler are putting the various things they have brought on the shelves.*

MR. KRALER. I'm sorry there is still so much confusion.

MR. FRANK. Please. Don't think of it. After all, we'll have plenty of leisure to arrange everything ourselves.

MIEP, *to Mrs. Frank.* We put the stores of food you sent in here. Your drugs are here . . . soap, linen here.

MRS. FRANK. Thank you, Miep.

MIEP. I made up the beds . . . the way Mr. Frank and Mr. Kraler said. *She starts out.* Forgive me. I have to hurry. I've got to go to the other side of town to get some ration books for you.

MRS. VAN DAAN.   Ration books? If they see our names on ration books, they'll know we're here.

MR. KRALER.   There isn't anything . . .

MIEP.   Don't worry. Your names won't be on them. *As she hurries out.* I'll be up later.   } *Together*

MR. FRANK.   Thank you, Miep.

MRS. FRANK, *to Mr. Kraler.* It's illegal, then, the ration books? We've never done anything illegal.

MR. FRANK.   We won't be living here exactly according to regulations. *As Mr. Kraler reassures Mrs. Frank, he takes various small things, such as matches, soap, etc., from his pockets, handing them to her.*

MR. KRALER.   This isn't the black market, Mrs. Frank. This is what we call the white market . . . helping all of the hundreds and hundreds who are hiding out in Amsterdam. *The carillon is heard playing the quarter-hour before eight. Mr. Kraler looks at his watch. Anne stops at the window as she comes down the stairs.*

ANNE.   It's the Westertoren!

MR. KRALER.   I must go. I must be out of here and downstairs in the office before the workmen get here. *He starts for the stairs leading out.* Miep or I, or both of us, will be up each day to bring you food and news and find out what your needs are. Tomorrow I'll get you a better bolt for the door at the foot of the stairs. It needs a bolt that you can throw yourself and open only at our signal. *To Mr. Frank.* Oh . . . You'll tell them about the noise?

MR. FRANK.   I'll tell them.

MR. KRALER.   Good-bye then for the moment. I'll come up again, after the workmen leave.

MR. FRANK.   Good-bye, Mr. Kraler.

MRS. FRANK, *shaking his hand.*   How can we thank you? *The others murmur their good-byes.*

MR. KRALER.   I never thought I'd live to see the day when a man like Mr. Frank would have to go into hiding. When you think—*He breaks off, going out. Mr. Frank follows him down the steps, bolting the door after him. In the interval before he returns, Peter goes over to Margot, shaking hands with her.*

*As Mr. Frank comes back up the steps, Mrs. Frank questions
him anxiously.*

MRS. FRANK. What did he mean, about the noise?

MR. FRANK. First let us take off some of these clothes. *They
all start to take off garment after garment. On each of their
coats, sweaters, blouses, suits, dresses, is another yellow Star of
David. Mr. and Mrs. Frank are under-dressed quite simply.
The others wear several things, sweaters, extra dresses, bath-
robes, aprons, nightgowns, etc.*

MR. VAN DAAN. It's a wonder we weren't arrested, walking
along the streets .`. . Petronella with a fur coat in July . . .
and that cat of Peter's crying all the way.

ANNE, *as she is removing a pair of panties.* A cat?

MRS. FRANK, *shocked.* Anne, please!

ANNE. It's all right. I've got on three more. *She pulls off two
more. Finally, as they have all removed their surplus clothes,
they look to Mr. Frank, waiting for him to speak.*

MR. FRANK. Now. About the noise. While the men are in the
building below, we must have complete quiet. Every sound can
be heard down there, not only in the workrooms, but in the
offices too. The men come at about eight-thirty, and leave at
about five-thirty. So, to be perfectly safe, from eight in the
morning until six in the evening we must move only when it is
necessary, and then in stockinged feet. We must not speak
above a whisper. We must not run any water. We cannot use the
sink, or even, forgive me, the w.c. The pipes go down through
the workrooms. It would be heard. No trash . . . *Mr. Frank
stops abruptly as he hears the sound of marching feet from the
street below. Everyone is motionless, paralyzed with fear. Mr.
Frank goes quietly into the room on the right to look down out
of the window. Anne runs after him, peering out with him.
The tramping feet pass without stopping. The tension is relieved. Mr. Frank, followed by Anne, returns to the main room
and resumes his instructions to the group . . .* No trash must
ever be thrown out which might reveal that someone is living
up here . . . not even a potato paring. We must burn everything in the stove at night. This is the way we must live until it
is over, if we are to survive. *There is silence for a second.*

MRS. FRANK. Until it is over.

MR. FRANK, *reassuringly.* After six we can move about . . . we can talk and laugh and have our supper and read and play games . . . just as we would at home. *He looks at his watch.* And now I think it would be wise if we all went to our rooms, and were settled before eight o'clock. Mrs. van Daan, you and your husband will be upstairs. I regret that there's no place up there for Peter. But he will be here, near us. This will be our common room, where we'll meet to talk and eat and read, like one family.

MR. VAN DAAN.   And where do you and Mrs. Frank sleep?

MR. FRANK.   This room is also our bedroom.

MRS. VAN DAAN.   That isn't right. We'll sleep here and you take the room upstairs.   } *Together*

MR. VAN DAAN.   It's your place.

MR. FRANK.   Please. I've thought this out for weeks. It's the best arrangement. The only arrangement.

MRS. VAN DAAN, *to Mr. Frank.* Never, never can we thank you. *Then to Mrs. Frank.* I don't know what would have happened to us, if it hadn't been for Mr. Frank.

MR. FRANK.   You don't know how your husband helped me when I came to this country . . . knowing no one . . . not able to speak the language. I can never repay him for that. *Going to van Daan.* May I help you with your things?

MR. VAN DAAN.   No. No. *To Mrs. van Daan.* Come along, *liefje.*

MRS. VAN DAAN.   You'll be all right. Peter? You're not afraid?

PETER, *embarrassed.* Please, Mother. *They start up the stairs to the attic room above. Mr. Frank turns to Mrs. Frank.*

MR. FRANK.   You too must have some rest, Edith. You didn't close your eyes last night. Nor you, Margot.

ANNE.   I slept, Father. Wasn't that funny? I knew it was the last night in my own bed, and yet I slept soundly.

MR. FRANK.   I'm glad, Anne. Now you'll be able to help me straighten things in here. *To Mrs. Frank and Margot.* Come with me . . . You and Margot rest in this room for the time being. *He picks up their clothes, starting for the room on the right.*

MRS. FRANK.   You're sure . . . ? I could help . . . And Anne hasn't had her milk . . .

MR. FRANK. I'll give it to her. *To Anne and Peter.* Anne, Peter . . . it's best that you take off your shoes now, before you forget. *He leads the way to the room, followed by Margot.*

MRS. FRANK. You're sure you're not tired, Anne?

ANNE. I feel fine. I'm going to help Father.

MRS. FRANK. Peter, I'm glad you are to be with us.

PETER. Yes, Mrs. Frank. *Mrs. Frank goes to join Mr. Frank and Margot.*

During the following scene Mr. Frank helps Margot and Mrs. Frank to hang up their clothes. Then he persuades them both to lie down and rest. The van Daans in their room above settle themselves. In the main room Anne and Peter remove their shoes. Peter takes his cat out of the carrier.

ANNE. What's your cat's name?

PETER. Mouschi.

ANNE. Mouschi! Mouschi! Mouschi! *She picks up the cat, walking away with it. To Peter.* I love cats. I have one . . . a darling little cat. But they made me leave her behind. I left some food and a note for the neighbours to take care of her . . . I'm going to miss her terribly. What is yours? A him or a her?

PETER. He's a tom. He doesn't like strangers. *He takes the cat from her, putting it back in its carrier.*

ANNE, *unabashed.* Then I'll have to stop being a stranger, won't I? Is he fixed?

PETER, *startled.* Huh?

ANNE. Did you have him fixed?

PETER. No.

ANNE. Oh, you ought to have him fixed—to keep him from—you know, fighting. Where did you go to school?

PETER. Jewish Secondary.

ANNE. But that's where Margot and I go! I never saw you around.

PETER. I used to see you . . . sometimes . . .

ANNE. You did?

PETER. . . . in the school yard. You were always in the middle of a bunch of kids. *He takes a penknife from his pocket.*

ANNE. Why didn't you ever come over?

PETER.   I'm sort of a lone wolf. *He starts to rip off his Star of David.*

ANNE.   What are you doing?

PETER.   Taking it off.

ANNE.   But you can't do that. They'll arrest you if you go out without your star. *He tosses his knife on the table.*

PETER.   Who's going out?

ANNE.   Why, of course! You're right! Of course we don't need them any more. *She picks up his knife and starts to take her star off.* I wonder what our friends will think when we don't show up today?

PETER.   I didn't have any dates with anyone.

ANNE.   Oh, I did. I had a date with Jopie to go and play ping-pong at her house. Do you know Jopie de Waal?

PETER.   No.

ANNE.   Jopie's my best friend. I wonder what she'll think when she telephones and there's no answer? . . . Probably she'll go over to the house . . . I wonder what she'll think . . . we left everything as if we'd suddenly been called away . . . breakfast dishes in the sink . . . beds not made . . . *As she pulls off her star the cloth underneath shows clearly the colour and form of the star.* Look! It's still there! *Peter goes over to the stove with his star.* What're you going to do with yours?

PETER.   Burn it.

ANNE, *she starts to throw hers in, and cannot.*   It's funny, I can't throw mine away. I don't know why.

PETER.   You can't throw . . . ? Something they branded you with . . . ? That they made you wear so they could spit on you?

ANNE.   I know. I know. But after all, it *is* the Star of David, isn't it? *In the bedroom, right, Margot and Mrs. Frank are lying down. Mr. Frank starts quietly out.*

PETER.   Maybe it's different for a girl. *Mr. Frank comes into the main room.*

MR. FRANK.   Forgive me, Peter. Now let me see. We must find a bed for your cat. *He goes to a cupboard.* I'm glad you brought your cat. Anne was feeling so badly about hers. *Getting a used small washtub.* Here we are. Will it be comfortable in that?

PETER, *gathering up his things.* Thanks.

MR. FRANK, *opening the door of the room on the left.* And here is your room. But I warn you, Peter, you can't grow any more. Not an inch, or you'll have to sleep with your feet out of the skylight. Are you hungry?

PETER. No.

MR. FRANK. We have some bread and butter.

PETER. No, thank you.

MR. FRANK. You can have it for luncheon then. And tonight we will have a real supper . . . our first supper together.

PETER. Thanks. Thanks. *He goes into his room. During the following scene he arranges his possessions in his new room.*

MR. FRANK. That's a nice boy, Peter.

ANNE. He's awfully shy, isn't he?

MR. FRANK. You'll like him, I know.

ANNE. I certainly hope so, since he's the only boy I'm likely to see for months and months. *Mr. Frank sits down, taking off his shoes.*

MR. FRANK. Annele, there's a box there. Will you open it? *He indicates a carton on the couch. Anne brings it to the centre table. In the street below there is the sound of children playing.*

ANNE, *as she opens the carton.* You know the way I'm going to think of it here? I'm going to think of it as a boarding house. A very peculiar summer boarding house, like the one that we —*She breaks off as she pulls out some photographs.* Father! My movie stars! I was wondering where they were! I was looking for them this morning . . . and Queen Wilhelmina! How wonderful!

MR. FRANK. There's something more. Go on. Look further. *He goes over to the sink, pouring a glass of milk from a thermos bottle.*

ANNE, *pulling out a pasteboard-bound book.* A diary! *She throws her arms around her father.* I've never had a diary. And I've always longed for one. *She looks around the room.* Pencil,

pencil, pencil, pencil. *She starts down the stairs.* I'm going down to the office to get a pencil.

MR. FRANK.   Anne! No! *He goes after her, catching her by the arm and pulling her back.*

ANNE, *startled.*   But there's no one in the building now.

MR. FRANK.   It doesn't matter. I don't want you ever to go beyond that door.

ANNE, *sobered.*   Never . . . ? Not even at night-time, when everyone is gone? Or on Sundays? Can't I go down to listen to the radio?

MR. FRANK.   Never. I am sorry, Anneke. It isn't safe. No, you must never go beyond that door. *For the first time Anne realizes what "going into hiding" means.*

ANNE.   I see.

MR. FRANK.   It'll be hard, I know. But always remember this, Anneke. There are no walls, there are no bolts, no locks that anyone can put on your mind. Miep will bring us books. We will read history, poetry, mythology. *He gives her the glass of milk.* Here's your milk. *With his arm about her, they go over to the couch, sitting down side by side.* As a matter of fact, between us, Anne, being here has certain advantages for you. For instance, you remember the battle you had with your mother the other day on the subject of overshoes? You said you'd rather die than wear overshoes? But in the end you had to wear them? Well now, you see, for as long as we are here you will never have to wear overshoes! Isn't that good? And the coat that you inherited from Margot, you won't have to wear that any more. And the piano! You won't have to practise on the piano. I tell you, this is going to be a fine life for you! *Anne's panic is gone. Peter appears in the doorway of his room, with a saucer in his hand. He is carrying his cat.*

PETER.   I . . . I . . . I thought I'd better get some water for Mouschi before . . .

MR. FRANK.   Of course. *As he starts toward the sink the carillon begins to chime the hour of eight. He tiptoes to the window at the back and looks down at the street below. He turns to Peter, indicating in pantomime that it is too late. Peter starts back for his room. He steps on a creaking board. The three of them are frozen for a minute in fear. As Peter starts away again,*

Anne tiptoes over to him and pours some of the milk from her glass into the saucer for the cat. Peter squats on the floor, putting the milk before the cat. Mr. Frank gives Anne his fountain pen, and then goes into the room at the right. For a second Anne watches the cat, then she goes over to the centre table, and opens her diary.

In the room at the right, Mrs. Frank has sat up quickly at the sound of the carillon. Mr. Frank comes in and sits down beside her on the settee, his arm comfortingly around her.

Upstairs, in the attic room, Mr. and Mrs. van Daan have hung their clothes in the closet and are now seated on the iron bed. Mrs. van Daan leans back exhausted. Mr. van Daan fans her with a newspaper.

Anne starts to write in her diary. The lights dim out, the curtain falls.

In the darkness Anne's voice comes to us again, faintly at first, and then with growing strength.

ANNE'S VOICE.   I expect I should be describing what it feels like to go into hiding. But I really don't know yet myself. I only know it's funny never to be able to go outdoors . . . never to breathe fresh air . . . never to run and shout and jump. It's the silence in the nights that frightens me most. Every time I hear a creak in the house, or a step on the street outside, I'm sure they're coming for us. The days aren't so bad. At least we know that Miep and Mr. Kraler are down there below us in the office. Our protectors, we call them. I asked Father what would happen to them if the Nazis found out they were hiding us. Pim said that they would suffer the same fate that we would . . . Imagine! They know this, and yet when they come up here, they're always cheerful and gay as if there were nothing in the world to bother them . . . Friday, the twenty-first of August, nineteen forty-two. Today I'm going to tell you our general news. Mother is unbearable. She insists on treating me like a baby, which I loathe. Otherwise things are going better. The weather is . . . *As Anne's voice is fading out, the curtain rises on the scene.*

SCENE 3

*It is a little after six o'clock in the evening, two months later.
Margot is in the bedroom at the right, studying. Mr. van Daan
is lying down in the attic room above.
The rest of the "family" is in the main room. Anne and Peter
sit opposite each other at the centre table, where they have been
doing their lessons. Mrs. Frank is on the couch. Mrs. van Daan
is seated with her fur coat, on which she has been sewing, in
her lap. None of them are wearing their shoes.
Their eyes are on Mr. Frank, waiting for him to give them the
signal which will release them from their day-long quiet. Mr.
Frank, his shoes in his hand, stands looking down out of the
window at the back, watching to be sure that all of the workmen have left the building below.
After a few seconds of motionless silence, Mr. Frank turns from
the window.*

MR. FRANK, *quietly, to the group.*   It's safe now. The last
workman has left. *There is an immediate stir of relief.*

ANNE, *her pent-up energy explodes.*   WHEE!

MRS. FRANK, *startled, amused.*   Anne!

MRS. VAN DAAN.   I'm first for the w.c. *She hurries off to the
bathroom. Mrs. Frank puts on her shoes and starts up to the
sink to prepare supper. Anne sneaks Peter's shoes from under
the table and hides them behind her back. Mr. Frank goes into
Margot's room.*

MR. FRANK, *to Margot.*   Six o'clock. School's over. *Margot
gets up, stretching. Mr. Frank sits down to put on his shoes. In
the main room Peter tries to find his.*

PETER, *to Anne.*   Have you seen my shoes?

ANNE, *innocently.*   Your shoes?

PETER.   You've taken them, haven't you?

ANNE.   I don't know what you're talking about.

PETER.   You're going to be sorry!

ANNE.   Am I? *Peter goes after her. Anne, with his shoes in her
hand, runs from him, dodging behind her mother.*

MRS. FRANK, *protesting.*   Anne, dear!

PETER.   Wait till I get you!

ANNE.   I'm waiting! *Peter makes a lunge for her. They both fall to the floor. Peter pins her down, wrestling with her to get the shoes.* Don't! Don't! Peter, stop it. Ouch!

MRS. FRANK.   Anne! . . . Peter! *Suddenly Peter becomes self-conscious. He grabs his shoes roughly and starts for his room.* ANNE, *following him.* Peter, where are you going? Come dance with me.

PETER.   I tell you I don't know how.

ANNE.   I'll teach you.

PETER.   I'm going to give Mouschi his dinner.

ANNE.   Can I watch?

PETER.   He doesn't like people around while he eats.

ANNE.   Peter, please.

PETER.   No! *He goes into his room. Anne slams his door after him.*

MRS. FRANK.   Anne, dear, I think you shouldn't play like that with Peter. It's not dignified.

ANNE.   Who cares if it's dignified? I don't want to be dignified. *Mr. Frank and Margot come from the room on the right. Margot goes to help her mother. Mr. Frank starts for the centre table to correct Margot's school papers.*

MRS. FRANK, *to Anne.*   You complain that I don't treat you like a grownup. But when I do, you resent it.

ANNE.   I only want some fun . . . someone to laugh and clown with . . . After you've sat still all day and hardly moved, you've got to have some fun. I don't know what's the matter with that boy.

MR. FRANK.   He isn't used to girls. Give him a little time.

ANNE.   Time? Isn't two months time? I could cry. *Catching hold of Margot.* Come on, Margot . . . dance with me. Come on, please.

MARGOT.   I have to help with supper.

ANNE.   You know we're going to forget how to dance . . . When we get out we won't remember a thing. *She starts to sing and dance by herself. Mr. Frank takes her in his arms, waltzing with her. Mrs. van Daan comes in from the bathroom.*

MRS. VAN DAAN.   Next? *She looks around as she starts putting on her shoes.* Where's Peter?

ANNE, *as they are dancing.*   Where would he be!

MRS. VAN DAAN.   He hasn't finished his lessons, has he? His father'll kill him if he catches him in there with that cat and his work not done. *Mr. Frank and Anne finish their dance. They bow to each other with extravagant formality.* Anne, get him out of there, will you?

ANNE, *at Peter's door.*   Peter? Peter?

PETER, *opening the door a crack.*   What is it?

ANNE.   Your mother says to come out.

PETER.   I'm giving Mouschi his dinner.

MRS. VAN DAAN.   You know what your father says. *She sits on the couch, sewing on the lining of her fur coat.*

PETER.   For heaven's sake, I haven't even looked at him since lunch.

MRS. VAN DAAN.   I'm just telling you, that's all.

ANNE.   I'll feed him.

PETER.   I don't want you in there.

MRS. VAN DAAN.   Peter!

PETER, *to Anne.*   Then give him his dinner and come right out, you hear? *He comes back to the table. Anne shuts the door of Peter's room after her and disappears behind the curtain covering his closet.*

MRS. VAN DAAN, *to Peter.*   Now is that any way to talk to your little girl friend?

PETER.   Mother . . . for heaven's sake . . . will you please stop saying that?

MRS. VAN DAAN.   Look at him blush! Look at him!

PETER.   Please! I'm not . . . anyway . . . let me alone, will you?

MRS. VAN DAAN.   He acts like it was something to be ashamed of. It's nothing to be ashamed of, to have a little girl friend.

PETER.   You're crazy. She's only thirteen.

MRS. VAN DAAN.   So what? And you're sixteen. Just perfect. Your father's ten years older than I am. *To Mr. Frank.* I warn you, Mr. Frank, if this war lasts much longer, we're going to be related and then . . .

MR. FRANK.   *Mazeltov!*

MRS. FRANK, *deliberately changing the conversation.*   I wonder where Miep is. She's usually so prompt. *Suddenly every-thing else is forgotten as they hear the sound of an automobile coming to a screeching stop in the street below. They are tense, motionless in their terror. The car starts away. A wave of relief sweeps over them. They pick up their occupations again. Anne flings open the door of Peter's room, making a dramatic en-trance. She is dressed in Peter's clothes. Peter looks at her in fury. The others are amused.*

ANNE.   Good evening, everyone. Forgive me if I don't stay. *She jumps up on a chair.* I have a friend waiting for me in there. My friend Tom. Tom Cat. Some people say that we look alike. But Tom has the most beautiful whiskers, and I have only a little fuzz. I am hoping . . . in time . . .

PETER.   All right, Mrs. Quack Quack!

ANNE, *outraged—jumping down.*   Peter!

PETER.   I heard about you . . . How you talked so much in class they called you Mrs. Quack Quack. How Mr. Smitter made you write a composition . . . " 'Quack, quack,' said Mrs. Quack Quack."

ANNE.   Well, go on. Tell them the rest. How it was so good he read it out loud to the class and then read it to all his other classes!

Peter.   Quack! Quack! Quack . . . Quack . . . Quack . . . *Anne pulls off the coat and trousers.*

ANNE.   You are the most intolerable, insufferable boy I've ever met! *She throws the clothes down the stairwell. Peter goes down after them.*

PETER.   Quack, quack, quack!

MRS. VAN DAAN, *to Anne.*   That's right, Anneke! Give it to him!

ANNE.   With all the boys in the world . . . Why I had to get locked up with one like you! . . .

PETER.   Quack, quack, quack, and from now on stay out of my room!

As Peter passes her, Anne puts out her foot, tripping him. He picks himself up, and goes on into his room.

MRS. FRANK, *quietly.*   Anne, dear . . . your hair. *She feels Anne's forehead.* You're warm. Are you feeling all right?

ANNE. Please, Mother.

She goes over to the centre table, slipping into her shoes.

MRS. FRANK, *following her.* You haven't a fever, have you?

ANNE, *pulling away.* No. No.

MRS. FRANK. You know we can't call a doctor here, ever. There's only one thing to do . . . watch carefully. Prevent an illness before it comes. Let me see your tongue.

ANNE. Mother, this is perfectly absurd.

MRS. FRANK. Anne, dear, don't be such a baby. Let me see your tongue. *As Anne refuses, Mrs. Frank appeals to Mr. Frank. Otto . . . ?*

MR. FRANK. You hear your mother, Anne. *Anne flicks out her tongue for a second, then turns away.*

MRS. FRANK. Come on—open up! *As Anne opens her mouth very wide.* You seem all right . . . but perhaps an aspirin . . .

MRS. VAN DAAN. For heaven's sake, don't give that child any pills. I waited for fifteen minutes this morning for her to come out of the w.c.

ANNE. I was washing my hair!

MR. FRANK. I think there's nothing the matter with our Anne that a ride on her bike, or a visit with her friend Jopie de Waal wouldn't cure. Isn't that so, Anne? *Mr. van Daan comes down into the room. From outside we hear faint sounds of bombers going over and a burst of ack-ack.*

MR. VAN DAAN. Miep not come yet?

MRS. VAN DAAN. The workmen just left, a little while ago.

MR. VAN DAAN. What's for dinner tonight?

MRS. VAN DAAN. Beans.

MR. VAN DAAN. Not again!

MRS. VAN DAAN. Poor Putti! I know. But what can we do? That's all that Miep brought us. *Mr. van Daan starts to pace, his hands behind his back. Anne follows behind him, imitating him.*

ANNE. We are now in what is known as the "bean cycle." Beans boiled, beans en casserole, beans with strings, beans without strings . . . *Peter has come out of his room. He slides into*

*his place at the table, becoming immediately absorbed in his
studies.*

MR. VAN DAAN, *to Peter.*   I saw you . . . in there, playing with
your cat.

MRS. VAN DAAN.   He just went in for a second, putting his coat
away. He's been out here all the time, doing his lessons.

MR. FRANK, *looking up from the papers.*   Anne, you got an
excellent in your history paper today . . . and very good in Latin.

ANNE, *sitting beside him.*   How about algebra?

MR. FRANK.   I'll have to make a confession. Up until now I've
managed to stay ahead of you in algebra. Today you caught up
with me. We'll leave it to Margot to correct.

ANNE.   Isn't algebra *vile,* Pim!

MR. FRANK.   Vile!

MARGOT, *to Mr. Frank.*   How did I do?

ANNE, *getting up.*   Excellent, excellent, excellent, excellent!

MR. FRANK, *to Margot.*   You should have used the subjunc-
tive here . . .

MARGOT.   Should I? . . . I thought . . . look here . . . I didn't use
it here . . . *The two become absorbed in the papers.*

ANNE.   Mrs. Van Daan, may I try on your coat?

MRS. FRANK.   No, Anne.

MRS. VAN DAAN, *giving it to Anne.*   It's all right . . . but careful with it. *Anne puts it on and struts with it.* My father gave
me that the year before he died. He always bought the best that
money could buy.

ANNE.   Mrs. Van Daan, did you have a lot of boy friends
before you were married?

MRS. FRANK.   Anne, that's a personal question. It's not courteous to ask personal questions.

MRS. VAN DAAN.   Oh I don't mind. *To Anne.* Our house was
always swarming with boys. When I was a girl we had . . .

MR. VAN DAAN.   Oh, God. Not again!

MRS. VAN DAAN, *good-humoured.*   Shut up! *Without a pause,
to Anne. Mr. van Daan mimics Mrs. van Daan, speaking the
first few words in unison with her.* One summer we had a big
house in Hilversum. The boys came buzzing round like bees
around a jam pot. And when I was sixteen! . . . We were wear-

ing our skirts very short those days and I had good-looking legs. *She pulls up her skirt, going to Mr. Frank.* I still have 'em. I may not be as pretty as I used to be, but I still have my legs. How about it, Mr. Frank?

MR. VAN DAAN. All right. All right. We see them.

MRS. VAN DAAN. I'm not asking you. I'm asking Mr. Frank.

PETER. Mother, for heaven's sake.

MRS. VAN DAAN. Oh, I embarrass you, do I? Well, I just hope the girl you marry has as good. *Then to Anne.* My father used to worry about me, with so many boys hanging round. He told me, if any of them gets fresh, you say to him . . . "Remember, Mr. So-and-So, remember I'm a lady."

ANNE. "Remember, Mr. So-and-So, remember I'm a lady." *She gives Mrs. van Daan her coat.*

MR. VAN DAAN. Look at you, talking that way in front of her! Don't you know she puts it all down in that diary?

MRS. VAN DAAN. So, if she does? I'm only telling the truth! *Anne stretches out, putting her ear to the floor, listening to what is going on below. The sound of the bombers fades away.*

MRS. FRANK, *setting the table.* Would you mind, Peter, if I moved you over to the couch?

ANNE, *listening.* Miep must have the radio on. *Peter picks up his papers, going over to the couch beside Mrs. van Daan.*

MR. VAN DAAN, *accusingly, to Peter.* Haven't you finished yet?

PETER. No.

MR. VAN DAAN. You ought to be ashamed of yourself.

PETER. All right. All right. I'm a dunce. I'm a hopeless case. Why do I go on?

MRS. VAN DAAN. You're not hopeless. Don't talk that way. It's just that you haven't anyone to help you, like the girls have. *To Mr. Frank.* Maybe you could help him, Mr. Frank?

MR. FRANK. I'm sure that his father . . . ?

MR. VAN DAAN. Not me. I can't do anything with him. He won't listen to me. You go ahead . . . if you want.

MR. FRANK, *going to Peter.* What about it, Peter? Shall we make our school coeducational?

MRS. VAN DAAN, *kissing Mr. Frank.* You're an angel, Mr. Frank. An angel. I don't know why I didn't meet you before I met that one there. Here, sit down, Mr. Frank . . . *She forces him down on the couch beside Peter.* Now Peter, you listen to Mr. Frank.

MR. FRANK.   It might be better for us to go into Peter's room. *Peter jumps up eagerly, leading the way.*

MRS. VAN DAAN.   That's right. You go in there, Peter. You listen to Mr. Frank. Mr. Frank is a highly educated man. *As Mr. Frank is about to follow Peter into his room, Mrs. Frank stops him and wipes the lipstick from his lips. Then she closes the door after them.*

ANNE, *on the floor, listening.*   Shh! I can hear a man's voice talking.

MR. VAN DAAN, *to Anne.*   Isn't it bad enough here without your sprawling all over the place? *Anne sits up.*

MRS. VAN DAAN, *to Mr. van Daan.*   If you didn't smoke so much, you wouldn't be so bad-tempered.

MR. VAN DAAN.   Am I smoking? Do you see me smoking?

MRS. VAN DAAN.   Don't tell me you've used up all those cigarettes.

MR. VAN DAAN.   One package. Miep only brought me one package.

MRS. VAN DAAN.   It's a filthy habit anyway. It's a good time to break yourself.

MR. VAN DAAN.   Oh, stop it, please.

MRS. VAN DAAN.   You're smoking up all our money. You know that, don't you?

MR. VAN DAAN.   Will you shut up? *During this, Mrs. Frank and Margot have studiously kept their eyes down. But Anne, seated on the floor, has been following the discussion interestedly. Mr. van Daan turns to see her staring up at him.* And what are you staring at?

ANNE.   I never heard grownups quarrel before. I thought only children quarrelled.

MR. VAN DAAN.   This isn't a quarrel! It's a discussion. And I never heard children so rude before.

ANNE, *rising, indignantly.*   I, rude!

MR. VAN DAAN.   Yes!

MRS. FRANK, *quickly.*   Anne, will you get me my knitting? *Anne goes to get it.* I must remember, when Miep comes, to ask her to bring me some more wool.

MARGOT, *going to her room.* I need some hairpins and some soap. I made a list. *She goes into her bedroom to get the list.*

MRS. FRANK, *to Anne.*   Have you some library books for Miep when she comes?

ANNE.   It's a wonder that Miep has a life of her own, the way we make her run errands for us. Please, Miep, get me some starch. Please take my hair out and have it cut. Tell me all the latest news, Miep. *She goes over, kneeling on the couch beside Mrs. van Daan.* Did you know she was engaged? His name is Dirk, and Miep's afraid the Nazis will ship him off to Germany to work in one of their war plants. That's what they're doing with some of the young Dutchmen . . . they pick them up off the streets—

MR. VAN DAAN, *interrupting.*   Don't you ever get tired of talking? Suppose you try keeping still for five minutes. Just five minutes. *He starts to pace again. Again Anne follows him, mimicking him. Mrs. Frank jumps up and takes her by the arm up to the sink, and gives her a glass of milk.*

MRS. FRANK.   Come here, Anne. It's time for your glass of milk.

MR. VAN DAAN.   Talk, talk, talk. I never heard such a child. Where is my . . . ? Every evening it's the same, talk, talk, talk. *He looks around.* Where is my . . . ?

MRS. VAN DAAN.   What're you looking for?

MR. VAN DAAN.   My pipe. Have you seen my pipe?

MRS. VAN DAAN.   What good's a pipe? You haven't got any tobacco.

MR. VAN DAAN.   At least I'll have something to hold in my mouth! *Opening Margot's bedroom door.* Margot, have you seen my pipe?

MARGOT.   It was on the table last night. *Anne puts her glass of milk on the table and picks up his pipe, hiding it behind her back.*

MR. VAN DAAN.   I know. I know. Anne, did you see my pipe? . . . Anne!

MRS. FRANK.   Anne, Mr. van Daan is speaking to you.

ANNE.   Am I allowed to talk now?

MR. VAN DAAN.   You're the most aggravating . . . The trouble with you is, you've been spoiled. What you need is a good old-fashioned spanking.

ANNE, *mimicking Mrs. van Daan.*   "Remember, Mr. So-and-So, remember I'm a lady." *She thrusts the pipe into his mouth, then picks up her glass of milk.*

MR. VAN DAAN, *restraining himself with difficulty.*   Why aren't you nice and quiet like your sister Margot? Why do you have to show off all the time? Let me give you a little advice, young lady. Men don't like that kind of thing in a girl. You know that? A man likes a girl who'll listen to him once in a while . . . a domestic girl, who'll keep her house shining for her husband . . . who loves to cook and sew and . . .

ANNE.   I'd cut my throat first! I'd open my veins! I'm going to be remarkable! I'm going to Paris . . .

MR. VAN DAAN, *scoffingly.*   Paris!

ANNE.   . . . to study music and art.

MR. VAN DAAN.   Yeah! Yeah!

ANNE.   I'm going to be a famous dancer or singer . . . or something wonderful. *She makes a wide gesture, spilling the glass of milk on the fur coat in Mrs. van Daan's lap. Margot rushes quickly over with a towel. Anne tries to brush the milk off with her skirt.*

MRS. VAN DAAN.   Now look what you've done . . . you clumsy little fool! My beautiful fur coat my father gave me . . .

ANNE.   I'm so sorry.

MRS. VAN DAAN.   What do you care? It isn't yours . . . So go on, ruin it! Do you know what that coat cost? Do you? And now look at it! Look at it!

ANNE.   I'm very, very sorry.

MRS. VAN DAAN.   I could kill you for this. I could just kill you! *Mrs. van Daan goes up the stairs, clutching the coat. Mr. van Daan starts after her.*

MR. VAN DAAN.   Petronella . . . *liefje! Liefje!* . . . Come back . . . the supper . . . come back!

MRS. FRANK.   Anne, you must not behave in that way.

ANNE. It was an accident. Anyone can have an accident.

MRS. FRANK. I don't mean that. I mean the answering back. You must not answer back. They are our guests. We must always show the greatest courtesy to them. We're all living under terrible tension. *She stops as Margot indicates that van Daan can hear. When he is gone, she continues.* That's why we must control ourselves . . . You don't hear Margot getting into arguments with them, do you? Watch Margot. She's always courteous with them. Never familiar. She keeps her distance. And they respect her for it. Try to be like Margot.

ANNE. And have them walk all over me, the way they do her? No, thanks!

MRS. FRANK. I'm not afraid that anyone is going to walk all over you, Anne. I'm afraid for other people, that you'll walk on them. I don't know what happens to you, Anne. You are wild, self-willed. If I had ever talked to my mother as you talk to me . . .

ANNE. Things have changed. People aren't like that any more. "Yes, Mother." "No, Mother." "Anything you say, Mother." I've got to fight things out for myself! Make something of myself!

MRS. FRANK. It isn't necessary to fight to do it. Margot doesn't fight, and isn't she . . . ?

ANNE, *violently rebellious.* Margot! Margot! Margot! That's all I hear from everyone . . . how wonderful Margot is . . . "Why aren't you like Margot?"

MARGOT, *protesting.* Oh, come on, Anne, don't be so . . .

ANNE, *paying no attention.* Everything she does is right, and everything I do is wrong! I'm the goat around here! . . . You're all against me! . . . And you worst of all! *She rushes off into her room and throws herself down on the settee, stifling her sobs. Mrs. Frank sighs and starts toward the stove.*

MRS. FRANK, *to Margot.* Let's put the soup on the stove . . . if there's anyone who cares to eat. Margot, will you take the bread out? *Margot gets the bread from the cupboard.* I don't know how we can go on living this way . . . I can't say a word to Anne . . . she flies at me . . .

MARGOT. You know Anne. In half an hour she'll be out here, laughing and joking.

MRS. FRANK.   And . . . *She makes a motion upwards, indicating the van Daans* . . . I told your father it wouldn't work . . . but no . . . no . . . he had to ask them, he said . . . he owed it to him, he said. Well, he knows now that I was right! These quarrels! . . . This bickering!

MARGOT, *with a warning look.*   Shush. Shush. *The buzzer for the door sounds. Mrs. Frank gasps, startled.*

MRS. FRANK.   Every time I hear that sound, my heart stops!

MARGOT, *starting for Peter's door.*   It's Miep. *She knocks at the door. Father? Mr. Frank comes quickly from Peter's room.*

MR. FRANK.   Thank you, Margot. *As he goes down the steps to open the outer door.* Has everyone his list?

MARGOT.   I'll get my books. *Giving her mother a list.* Here's your list. *Margot goes into her and Anne's bedroom on the right. Anne sits up, hiding her tears, as Margot comes in.* Miep's here. *Margot picks up her books and goes back. Anne hurries over to the mirror, smoothing her hair.*

MR. VAN DAAN, *coming down the stairs.* Is it Miep?

MARGOT.   Yes. Father's gone down to let her in.

MR. VAN DAAN.   At last I'll have some cigarettes!

MRS. FRANK, *to Mr. van Daan.*   I can't tell you how unhappy I am about Mrs. van Daan's coat. Anne should never have touched it.

MR. VAN DAAN.   She'll be all right.

MRS. FRANK.   Is there anything I can do?

MR. VAN DAAN.   Don't worry. *He turns to meet Miep. But it is not Miep who comes up the steps. It is Mr. Kraler, followed by Mr. Frank. Their faces are grave. Anne comes from the bedroom. Peter comes from his room.*

MRS. FRANK.   Mr. Kraler!

MR. VAN DAAN.   How are you, Mr. Kraler?

MARGOT.   This is a surprise.

MRS. FRANK.   When Mr. Kraler comes, the sun begins to shine.

MR. VAN DAAN.   Miep is coming?

MR. KRALER.   Not tonight. *Kraler goes to Margot and Mrs. Frank and Anne, shaking hands with them.*

MRS. FRANK.   Wouldn't you like a cup of coffee? . . . Or, better still, will you have supper with us?

MR. FRANK.   Mr. Kraler has something to talk over with us. Something has happened, he says, which demands an immediate decision.

MRS. FRANK, *fearful.* What is it? *Mr. Kraler sits down on the couch. As he talks he takes bread, cabbages, milk, etc., from his briefcase, giving them to Margot and Anne to put away.*

MR. KRALER.   Usually, when I come up here, I try to bring you some bit of good news. What's the use of telling you the bad news when there's nothing that you can do about it? But today something has happened . . . Dirk . . . Miep's Dirk, you know, came to me just now. He tells me that he has a Jewish friend living near him. A dentist. He says he's in trouble. He begged me, could I do anything for this man? Could I find him a hiding place? . . . So I've come to you . . . I know it's a terrible thing to ask of you, living as you are, but would you take him in with you?

MR. FRANK.   Of course we will.

MR. KRALER, *rising.* It'll be just for a night or two . . . until I find some other place. This happened so suddenly that I didn't know where to turn.

MR. FRANK.   Where is he?

MR. KRALER.   Downstairs in the office.

MR. FRANK.   Good. Bring him up.

MR. KRALER.   His name is Dussel . . . Jan Dussel.

MR. FRANK.   Dussel . . . I think I know him.

MR. KRALER.   I'll get him. *He goes quickly down the steps and out. Mr. Frank suddenly becomes conscious of the others.*

MR. FRANK.   Forgive me. I spoke without consulting you. But I knew you'd feel as I do.

MR. VAN DAAN.   There's no reason for you to consult anyone. This is your place. You have a right to do exactly as you please. The only thing I feel . . . there's so little food as it is . . . and to take in another person . . . *Peter turns away, ashamed of his father.*

MR. FRANK.   We can stretch the food a little. It's only for a few days.

MR. VAN DAAN.   You want to make a bet?

MRS. FRANK.   I think it's fine to have him. But, Otto, where are you going to put him? Where?

PETER.   He can have my bed. I can sleep on the floor. I wouldn't mind.

MR. FRANK.   That's good of you, Peter. But your room's too small . . . even for *you*.

ANNE.   I have a much better idea. I'll come in here with you and Mother, and Margot can take Peter's room and Peter can go in our room with Mr. Dussel.

MARGOT.   That's right. We could do that.

MR. FRANK.   No, Margot. You mustn't sleep in that room . . . neither you nor Anne. Mouschi has caught some rats in there. Peter's brave. He doesn't mind.

ANNE.   Then how about *this?* I'll come in here with you and Mother, and Mr. Dussel can have my bed.

MRS. FRANK.   No. No. *No!* Margot will come in here with us and he can have her bed. It's the only way. Margot, bring your things in here. Help her, Anne. *Margot hurries into her room to get her things.*

ANNE, *to her mother.*   Why Margot?· Why can't I come in here?

MRS. FRANK.   Because it wouldn't be proper for Margot to sleep with a . . . Please, Anne. Don't argue. Please. *Anne starts slowly away.*

MR. FRANK, *to Anne.*   You don't mind sharing your room with Mr. Dussel, do you, Anne?

ANNE.   No. No, of course not.

MR. FRANK.   Good. *Anne goes off into her bedroom, helping Margot. Mr. Frank starts to search in the cupboards.* Where's the cognac?

MRS. FRANK.   It's there. But, Otto, I was saving it in case of illness.

MR. FRANK.   I think we couldn't find a better time to use it. Peter, will you get five glasses for me? *Peter goes for the glasses. Margot comes out of her bedroom, carrying her possessions, which she hangs behind a curtain in the main room. Mr. Frank finds the cognac and pours it into the five glasses that Peter brings him. Mr. van Daan stands looking on sourly. Mrs. van Daan comes downstairs and looks around at all the bustle.*

MRS. VAN DAAN.   What's happening? What's going on?

MR. VAN DAAN.   Someone's moving in with us.

MRS. VAN DAAN.   In here? You're joking.

MARGOT.   It's only for a night or two . . . until Mr. Kraler finds him another place.

MR. VAN DAAN.   Yeah! Yeah! *Mr. Frank hurries over as Mr. Kraler and Dussel come up. Dussel is a man in his late fifties, meticulous, finicky . . . bewildered now. He wears a raincoat. He carries a briefcase, stuffed full, and a small medicine case.*

MR. FRANK.   Come in, Mr. Dussel.

MR. KRALER.   This is Mr. Frank.

DUSSEL.   Mr. Otto Frank?

MR. FRANK.   Yes. Let me take your things. *He takes the hat and briefcase, but Dussel clings to his medicine case.* This is my wife Edith . . . Mr. and Mrs. van Daan . . . their son, Peter . . . and my daughters, Margot and Anne. *Dussel shakes hands with everyone.*

MR. KRALER.   Thank you, Mr. Frank. Thank you all. Mr. Dussel, I leave you in good hands. Oh . . . Dirk's coat. *Dussel hurriedly takes off the raincoat, giving it to Mr. Kraler. Underneath is his white dentist's jacket, with a yellow Star of David on it.*

DUSSEL, *to Mr. Kraler.*   What can I say to thank you . . . ?

MRS. FRANK, *to Dussel.*   Mr. Kraler and Miep . . . They're our lifeline. Without them we couldn't live.

MR. KRALER.   Please. Please. You make us seem very heroic. It isn't that at all. We simply don't like the Nazis. *To Mr. Frank, who offers him a drink.* No, thanks. *Then going on.* We don't like their methods. We don't like . . .

MR. FRANK, *smiling.*   I know. I know. "No one's going to tell us Dutchmen what to do with our damn Jews!"

MR. KRALER, *to Dussel.*   Pay no attention to Mr. Frank. I'll be up tomorrow to see that they're treating you right. *To Mr. Frank.* Don't trouble to come down again. Peter will bolt the door after me, won't you, Peter?

PETER.   Yes, sir.

MR. FRANK.   Thank you, Peter. I'll do it.

MR. KRALER.   Good night. Good night.

GROUP.   Good night, Mr. Kraler. We'll see you tomorrow, etc.,

Mr. Kraler goes out with Mr. Frank. Mrs. Frank gives each one of the "grownups" a glass of cognac.

MRS. FRANK. Please, Mr. Dussel, sit down.

Mr. Dussel sinks into a chair. Mrs. Frank gives him a glass of cognac.

DUSSEL. I'm dreaming. I know it. I can't believe my eyes. Mr. Otto Frank here! *To Mrs. Frank.* You're not in Switzerland then? A woman told me. . . . She said she'd gone to your house . . . the door was open, everything was in disorder, dishes in the sink. She said she found a piece of paper in the wastebasket with an address scribbled on it . . . an address in Zurich. She said you must have escaped to Zurich.

ANNE. Father put that there purposely . . . just so people would think that very thing!

DUSSEL. And you've been *here* all the time?

MRS. FRANK. All the time . . . ever since July. *Anne speaks to her father as he comes back.*

ANNE. It worked, Pim . . . the address you left! Mr. Dussel says that people believe we escaped to Switzerland.

MR. FRANK. I'm glad . . . And now let's have a little drink to welcome Mr. Dussel. *Before they can drink, Mr. Dussel bolts his drink. Mr. Frank smiles and raises his glass.* To Mr. Dussel. Welcome. We're very honoured to have you with us.

MRS. FRANK. To Mr. Dussel, welcome. *The van Daans murmur a welcome. The "grownups" drink.*

MRS. VAN DAAN. Um. That was good.

MR. VAN DAAN. Did Mr. Kraler warn you that you won't get much to eat here? You can imagine . . . three ration books among the seven of us . . . and now you make eight. *Peter walks away, humiliated. Outside, a street organ is heard dimly.*

DUSSEL, *rising.* Mr. van Daan, you don't realize what is happening outside that you should warn me of a thing like that. You don't realize what's going on. . . . *As Mr. van Daan starts his characteristic pacing, Dussel turns to speak to the others.* Right here in Amsterdam every day hundreds of Jews disappear . . . They surround a block and search house by house. Children come home from school to find their parents gone. Hundreds are being deported . . . people that you and I know . . . the Hallensteins . . . the Wessels . . .

MRS. FRANK, *in tears.* Oh, no. No!

DUSSEL. They get their call-up notice . . . come to the Jewish theatre on such and such a day and hour . . . bring only what you can carry in a rucksack. And if you refuse the call-up notice, then they come and drag you from your home and ship you off to Mauthausen. The death camp!

MRS. FRANK. We didn't know that things had got so much worse.

DUSSEL. Forgive me for speaking so.

ANNE, *coming to Dussel.* Do you know the de Waals? . . . What's become of them? Their daughter Jopie and I are in the same class. Jopie's my best friend.

DUSSEL. They are gone.

ANNE. Gone?

DUSSEL. With all the others.

ANNE. Oh, no. Not Jopie! *She turns away, in tears. Mrs. Frank motions to Margot to comfort her. Margot goes to Anne, putting her arms comfortingly around her.*

MRS. VAN DAAN. There were some people called Wagner. They lived near us . . . ?

MR. FRANK, *interrupting, with a glance at Anne.* I think we should put this off until later. We all have many questions we want to ask . . . But I'm sure that Mr. Dussel would like to get settled before supper.

DUSSEL. Thank you. I would. I brought very little with me.

MR. FRANK, *giving him his hat and briefcase.* I'm sorry we can't give you a room alone. But I hope you won't be too uncomfortable. We've had to make strict rules here . . . a schedule of hours . . . We'll tell you after supper. Anne, would you like to take Mr. Dussel to his room?

ANNE, *controlling her tears.* If you'll come with me, Mr. Dussel? *She starts for her room.*

DUSSEL, *shaking hands with each in turn.* Forgive me if I haven't really expressed my gratitude to all of you. This has been such a shock to me. I'd always thought of myself as Dutch. I was born in Holland. My father was born in Holland, and my grandfather. And now . . . after all these years . . . *He breaks off.* If you'll excuse me. *Dussel gives a little bow and hurries off after Anne. Mr. Frank and the others are subdued.*

ANNE, *turning on the light.* Well, here we are. *Dussel looks around the room. In the main room Margot speaks to her mother.*

MARGOT. The news sounds pretty bad, doesn't it? It's so different from what Mr. Kraler tells us. Mr. Kraler says things are improving.

MR. VAN DAAN. I like it better the way Kraler tells it. *They resume their occupations, quietly. Peter goes off into his room. In Anne's room, Anne turns to Dussel.*

ANNE. You're going to share the room with me.

DUSSEL. I'm a man who's always lived alone. I haven't had to adjust myself to others. I hope you'll bear with me until I learn.

ANNE. Let me help you. *She takes his briefcase.* Do you always live all alone? Have you no family at all?

DUSSEL. No one. *He opens his medicine case and spreads his bottles on the dressing table.*

ANNE. How dreadful. You must be terribly lonely.

DUSSEL. I'm used to it.

ANNE. I don't think I could ever get used to it. Didn't you even have a pet? A cat, or a dog?

DUSSEL. I have an allergy for fur-bearing animals. They give me asthma.

ANNE. Oh, dear. Peter has a cat.

DUSSEL. Here? He has it here?

ANNE. Yes. But we hardly ever see it. He keeps it in his room all the time. I'm sure it will be all right.

DUSSEL. Let us hope so. *He takes some pills to fortify himself.*

ANNE. That's Margot's bed, where you're going to sleep. I sleep on the sofa there. *Indicating the clothes hooks on the wall.* We cleared these off for your things. *She goes over to the window.* The best part about this room . . . you can look down and see a bit of the street and the canal. There's a houseboat . . . you can see the end of it . . . a bargeman lives there with his family . . . They have a baby and he's just beginning to walk and I'm so afraid he's going to fall into the canal some day. I watch him. . . .

DUSSEL, *interrupting.* Your father spoke of a schedule.

ANNE, *coming away from the window.* Oh, yes. It's mostly

about the times we have to be quiet. And times for the w.c. You can use it now if you like.

DUSSEL, *stiffly.* No, thank you.

ANNE. I suppose you think it's awful, my talking about a thing like that. But you don't know how important it can get to be, especially when you're frightened . . . About this room, the way Margot and I did . . . she had it to herself in the afternoons for studying, reading . . . lessons, you know . . . and I took the mornings. Would that be all right with you?

DUSSEL. I'm not at my best in the morning.

ANNE. You stay here in the mornings then. I'll take the room in the afternoons.

DUSSEL. Tell me, when you're in here, what happens to me? Where am I spending my time? In there, with all the people?

ANNE. Yes.

DUSSEL. I see. I see.

ANNE. We have supper at half past six.

DUSSEL, *going over to the sofa.* Then, if you don't mind . . . I like to lie down quietly for ten minutes before eating. I find it helps the digestion.

ANNE. Of course. I hope I'm not going to be too much of a bother to you. I seem to be able to get everyone's back up. *Dussel lies down on the sofa, curled up, his back to her.*

DUSSEL. I always get along very well with children. My patients all bring their children to me, because they know I get on well with them. So don't you worry about that. *Anne leans over him, taking his hand and shaking it gratefully.*

ANNE. Thank you. Thank you, Mr. Dussel. *The lights dim to darkness. The curtain falls on the scene. Anne's voice comes to us faintly at first, and then with increasing power.*

ANNE'S VOICE. . . . And yesterday I finished Cissy van Marxvelt's latest book. I think she is a first-class writer. I shall definitely let my children read her. Monday the twenty-first of September, nineteen forty-two. Mr. Dussel and I had another battle yesterday. Yes, Mr. Dussel! According to him, nothing, I repeat . . . nothing, is right about me . . . my appearance, my character, my manners. While he was going on at me I thought . . . sometime I'll give you such a smack that you'll fly right up

to the ceiling! Why is it that every grownup thinks he knows
the way to bring up children? Particularly the grownups that
never had any. I keep wishing that Peter was a girl instead of
a boy. Then I would have someone to talk to. Margot's a darling, but she takes everything too seriously. To pause for a
moment on the subject of Mrs. van Daan. I must tell you that
her attempts to flirt with father are getting her nowhere. Pim,
thank goodness, won't play. *As she is saying the last lines, the
curtain rises on the darkened scene. Anne's voice fades out.*

SCENE 4

*It is the middle of the night, several months later. The stage is
dark except for a little light which comes through the skylight
in Peter's room.*

*Everyone is in bed. Mr. and Mrs. Frank lie on the couch in the
main room, which has been pulled out to serve as a makeshift
double bed.*

*Margot is sleeping on a mattress on the floor in the main room,
behind a curtain stretched across for privacy. The others are all
in their accustomed rooms.*

From outside we hear two drunken soldiers singing "Lili Marlene." *A girl's high giggle is heard. The sound of running
feet is heard coming closer and then fading in the distance.
Throughout the scene there is the distant sound of airplanes
passing overhead.*

*A match suddenly flares up in the attic. We dimly see Mr. van
Daan. He is getting his bearings. He comes quickly down the
stairs, and goes to the cupboard where the food is stored. Again
the match flares up, and is as quickly blown out. The dim figure
is seen to steal back up the stairs.*

*There is quiet for a second or two, broken only by the sound of
airplanes, and running feet on the street below.*

Suddenly, out of the silence and the dark, we hear Anne scream.

ANNE, *screaming.*   No! No! Don't . . . don't take me! *She
moans, tossing and crying in her sleep. The other people
wake, terrified. Dussel sits up in bed, furious.*

Dussel. Shush! Anne! Anne, for God's sake, shush!

Anne, *still in her nightmare.* Save me! Save me! *She screams and screams. Dussel gets out of bed, going over to her, trying to wake her.*

Dussel. For God's sake! Quiet! Quiet! You want someone to hear? *In the main room Mrs. Frank grabs a shawl and pulls it around her. She rushes in to Anne, taking her in her arms. Mr. Frank hurriedly gets up, putting on his overcoat. Margot sits up, terrified. Peter's light goes on in his room.*

Mrs. Frank, *to Anne, in her room.* Hush, darling, hush. It's all right. It's all right. *Over her shoulder to Dussel.* Will you be kind enough to turn on the light, Mr. Dussel? *Back to Anne.* It's nothing, my darling. It was just a dream.

Dussel turns on the light in the bedroom. Mrs. Frank holds Anne in her arms. Gradually Anne comes out of her nightmare, still trembling with horror. Mr. Frank comes into the room, and goes quickly to the window, looking out to be sure that no one outside has heard Anne's screams. Mrs. Frank holds Anne, talking softly to her. In the main room Margot stands on a chair, turning on the centre hanging lamp. A light goes on in the van Daans' room overhead. Peter puts his robe on, coming out of his room.

Dussel, *to Mrs. Frank, blowing his nose.* Something must be done about that child, Mrs. Frank. Yelling like that! Who knows but there's somebody on the streets? She's endangering all our lives.

Mrs. Frank. Anne, darling.

Dussel. Every night she twists and turns. I don't sleep. I spend half my night shushing her. And now it's nightmares!

Margot comes to the door of Anne's room, followed by Peter. Mr. Frank goes to them, indicating that everything is all right. Peter takes Margot back.

Mrs. Frank, *to Anne.* You're here, safe, you see? Nothing has happened. *To Dussel.* Please, Mr. Dussel, go back to bed. She'll be herself in a minute or two. Won't you, Anne?

Dussel, *picking up a book and a pillow.* Thank you, but I'm going to the w.c. The one place where there's peace! *He stalks *out. Mr. van Daan, in underwear and trousers, comes down the stairs.*

MR. VAN DAAN, *to Dussel.* What is it? What happened?

DUSSEL. A nightmare. She was having a nightmare!

MR. VAN DAAN. I thought someone was murdering her.

DUSSEL. Unfortunately, no. *He goes into the bathroom. Mr. van Daan goes back up the stairs. Mr. Frank, in the main room, sends Peter back to his own bedroom.*

MR. FRANK. Thank you, Peter. Go back to bed.

Peter goes back to his room. Mr. Frank follows him, turning out the light and looking out the window. Then he goes back to the main room, and gets up on a chair, turning out the centre hanging lamp.

MRS. FRANK, *to Anne.* Would you like some water? *Anne shakes her head.* Was it a very bad dream? Perhaps if you told me . . . ?

ANNE. I'd rather not talk about it.

MRS. FRANK. Poor darling. Try to sleep then. I'll sit right here beside you until you fall asleep. *She brings a stool over, sitting there.*

ANNE. You don't have to.

MRS. FRANK. But I'd like to stay with you . . . very much. Really.

ANNE. I'd rather you didn't.

MRS. FRANK. Good night, then. *She leans down to kiss Anne. Anne throws her arm up over her face, turning away. Mrs. Frank, hiding her hurt, kisses Anne's arm.* You'll be all right? There's nothing that you want?

ANNE. Will you please ask Father to come.

MRS. FRANK, *after a second.* Of course, Anne dear.

She hurries out into the other room. Mr. Frank comes to her as she comes in. Sie verlangt nach Dir!

MR. FRANK, *sensing her hurt.* Edith, *Liebe, schau . . .*

MRS. FRANK. *Es macht nichts! Ich danke dem lieben Herrgott, dass sie sich wenigstens an Dich wendet, wenn sie Trost braucht! Geh hinein, Otto, sie ist ganz hysterisch vor Angst.*

As Mr. Frank hesitates. Geh zu ihr. He looks at her for a second and then goes to get a cup of water for Anne. Mrs. Frank sinks down on the bed, her face in her hands, trying to keep from sobbing aloud. Margot comes over to her, putting her arms around her. She wants nothing of me. She pulled away when I leaned down to kiss her.

MARGOT. It's a phase . . . You heard Father . . . Most girls go through it . . . they turn to their fathers at this age . . . they give all their love to their fathers.

MRS. FRANK. You weren't like this. You didn't shut me out.

MARGOT. She'll get over it . . .

She smooths the bed for Mrs. Frank and sits beside her a moment as Mrs. Frank lies down. In Anne's room Mr. Frank comes in, sitting down by Anne. Anne flings her arms around him, clinging to him. In the distance we hear the sound of ack-ack.

ANNE. Oh, Pim. I dreamed that they came to get us! The Green Police! They broke down the door and grabbed me and started to drag me out the way they did Jopie.

MR. FRANK. I want you to take this pill.

ANNE. What is it?

MR. FRANK. Something to quiet you. *She takes it and drinks the water. In the main room Margot turns out the light and goes back to her bed.*

MR. FRANK, *to Anne.* Do you want me to read to you for a while?

ANNE. No. Just sit with me for a minute. Was I awful? Did I yell terribly loud? Do you think anyone outside could have heard?

MR. FRANK. No. No. Lie quietly now. Try to sleep.

ANNE. I'm a terrible coward. I'm so disappointed in myself. I think I've conquered my fear . . . I think I'm really grown-up . . . and then something happens . . . and I run to you like a baby . . . I love you, Father. I don't love anyone but you.

MR. FRANK, *reproachfully.* Annele!

ANNE. It's true. I've been thinking about it for a long time. You're the only one I love.

MR. FRANK. It's fine to hear you tell me that you love me. But

I'd be happier if you said you loved your mother as well . . . She needs your help so much . . . your love . . .

ANNE.   We have nothing in common. She doesn't understand me. Whenever I try to explain my views on life to her she asks me if I'm constipated.

MR. FRANK.   You hurt her very much just now. She's crying. She's in there crying.

ANNE.   I can't help it. I only told the truth. I didn't want her here . . . *Then, with sudden change.* Oh, Pim, I was horrible, wasn't I? And the worst of it is, I can stand off and look at myself doing it and know it's cruel and yet I can't stop doing it. What's the matter with me? Tell me. Don't say it's just a phase! Help me.

MR. FRANK.   There is so little that we parents can do to help our children. We can only try to set a good example . . . point the way. The rest you must do yourself. You must build your own character.

ANNE.   I'm trying. Really I am. Every night I think back over all of the things I did that day that were wrong . . . like putting the wet mop in Mr. Dussel's bed . . . and this thing now with Mother. I say to myself, that was wrong. I make up my mind, I'm never going to do that again. Never! Of course I may do something worse . . . but at least I'll never do *that* again! . . . I have a nicer side, Father . . . a sweeter, nicer side. But I'm scared to show it. I'm afraid that people are going to laugh at me if I'm serious. So the mean Anne comes to the outside and the good Anne stays on the inside, and I keep on trying to switch them around and have the good Anne outside and the bad Anne inside and be what I'd like to be . . . and might be . . . if only . . . only . . . *She is asleep. Mr. Frank watches her for a moment and then turns off the light, and starts out. The lights dim out. The curtain falls on the scene. Anne's voice is heard dimly at first, and then with growing strength.*

ANNE'S VOICE.   . . . The air raids are getting worse. They come over day and night. The noise is terrifying. Pim says it should be music to our ears. The more planes, the sooner will come the end of the war. Mrs. van Daan pretends to be a fatalist. What will be, will be. But when the planes come over, who is the most frightened? No one else but Petronella! . . . Monday, the ninth of November, nineteen forty-two. Wonderful news!

The Allies have landed in Africa. Pim says that we can look for an early finish to the war. Just for fun he asked each of us what was the first thing we wanted to do when we got out of here. Mrs. van Daan longs to be home with her own things, her needle-point chairs, the Bechstein piano her father gave her . . . the best that money could buy. Peter would like to go to a movie. Mr. Dussel wants to get back to his dentist's drill. He's afraid he is losing his touch. For myself, there are so many things . . . to ride a bike again . . . to laugh till my belly aches . . . to have new clothes from the skin out . . . to have a hot tub filled to overflowing and wallow in it for hours . . . to be back in school with my friends. . . .

As the last lines are being said, the curtain rises on the scene. The lights dim on as Anne's voice fades away.

SCENE 5

It is the first night of the Hanukkah celebration. Mr. Frank is standing at the head of the table on which is the Menorah. He lights the Shamos, or servant candle, and holds it as he says the blessing. Seated listening is all of the "family," dressed in their best. The men wear hats, Peter wears his cap.

MR. FRANK, *reading from a prayer book.* "Praised be Thou, oh Lord our God, Ruler of the universe, who hast sanctified us with Thy commandments and bidden us kindle the Hanukkah lights. Praised be Thou, oh Lord our God, Ruler of the universe, who hast wrought wondrous deliverances for our fathers in days of old. Praised be Thou, oh Lord our God, Ruler of the universe, that Thou hast given us life and sustenance and brought us to this happy season." *Mr. Frank lights the one candle of the Menorah as he continues.* "We kindle this Hanukkah light to celebrate the great and wonderful deeds wrought through the zeal with which God filled the hearts of the heroic Maccabees, two thousand years ago. They fought against indifference, against tyranny and oppression, and they restored our Temple to us. May these lights remind us that we should ever look to God, whence cometh our help." Amen. [Pronounced O-mayn.]

ALL.   Amen. *Mr. Frank hands Mrs. Frank the prayer book.*

MRS. FRANK, *reading.*   "I lift up mine eyes unto the mountains, from whence cometh my help. My help cometh from the Lord who made heaven and earth. He will not suffer thy foot to to be moved. He that keepeth thee will not slumber. He that keepeth Israel doth neither slumber nor sleep. The Lord is thy keeper. The Lord is thy shade upon thy right hand. The sun shall not smite thee by day, nor the moon by night. The Lord shall keep thee from all evil. He shall keep thy soul. The Lord shall guard thy going out and thy coming in, from this time forth and forevermore." Amen.

ALL.   Amen.

Mrs. Frank puts down the prayer book and goes to get the food and wine. Margot helps her. Mr. Frank takes the men's hats and puts them aside.

DUSSEL, *rising.*   That was very moving.

ANNE, *pulling him back.*   It isn't over yet!

MRS. VAN DAAN.   Sit down! Sit down!

ANNE.   There's a lot more, songs and presents.

DUSSEL.   Presents?

MRS. FRANK.   Not this year, unfortunately.

MRS. VAN DAAN.   But always on Hanukkah everyone gives presents . . . everyone!

DUSSEL.   Like our St. Nicholas' Day. *There is a chorus of "no's" from the group.*

MRS. VAN DAAN.   No! Not like St. Nicholas! What kind of a Jew are you that you don't know Hanukkah?

MRS. FRANK, *as she brings the food.*   I remember particularly the candles . . . First one, as we have tonight. Then the second night you light two candles, the next night three . . . and so on until you have eight candles burning. When there are eight candles it is truly beautiful.

MRS. VAN DAAN.   And the potato pancakes.

MR. VAN DAAN.   Don't talk about them!

MRS. VAN DAAN.   I make the best *latkes* you ever tasted!

MRS. FRANK.   Invite us all next year . . . in your own home.

MR. FRANK.   God willing!

MRS. VAN DAAN.   God willing.

MARGOT.   What I remember best is the presents we used to get when we were little . . . eight days of presents . . . and each day they got better and better.

MRS. FRANK, *sitting down.*   We are all here, alive. That is present enough.

ANNE.   No, it isn't. I've got something . . . *She rushes into her room, hurriedly puts on a little hat improvised from the lamp shade, grabs a satchel bulging with parcels and comes running back.*

MRS. FRANK.   What is it?

ANNE.   Presents!

MRS. VAN DAAN.   Presents!

DUSSEL.   Look!

MR. VAN DAAN.   What's she got on her head?

PETER.   A lamp shade!

ANNE, *she picks out one at random.*   This is for Margot. *She hands it to Margot, pulling her to her feet.* Read it out loud.

MARGOT, *reading.*   "You have never lost your temper.
        You never will, I fear,
        You are so good.
        But if you should,
        Put all your cross words here."

She tears open the package. A new crossword puzzle book! Where did you get it?

ANNE.   It isn't new. It's one that you've done. But I rubbed it all out, and if you wait a little and forget, you can do it all over again.

MARGOT, *sitting.*   It's wonderful, Anne. Thank you. You'd never know it wasn't new. *From outside we hear the sound of a street-car passing.*

ANNE, *with another gift.*   Mrs. van Daan.

MRS. VAN DAAN, *taking it.*   This is awful . . . I haven't anything for anyone . . . I never thought . . .

MR. FRANK.   This is all Anne's idea.

MRS. VAN DAAN, *holding up a bottle.*   What is it?

ANNE.   It's hair shampoo. I took all the odds and ends of soap and mixed them with the last of my toilet water.

MRS. VAN DAAN.   Oh, Anneke!

ANNE.   I wanted to write a poem for all of them, but I didn't have time. *Offering a large box to Mr. van Daan.* Yours, Mr. van Daan, is *really* something . . . something you want more than anything. *As she waits for him to open it.* Look! Cigarettes!

MR. VAN DAAN.   Cigarettes!

ANNE.   Two of them! Pim found some old pipe tobacco in the pocket lining of his coat . . . and we made them . . . or rather, Pim did.

MRS. VAN DAAN.   Let me see . . . Well, look at that! Light it, Putti! Light it. *Mr. van Daan hesitates.*

ANNE.   It's tobacco, really it is! There's a little fluff in it, but not much. *Everyone watches intently as Mr. van Daan cautiously lights it. The cigarette flares up. Everyone laughs.*

PETER.   It works!

MRS. VAN DAAN.   Look at him.

MR. VAN DAAN, *spluttering.*   Thank you, Anne. Thank you. *Anne rushes back to her satchel for another present.*

ANNE, *handing her mother a piece of paper.*   For Mother, Hanukkah greeting. *She pulls her mother to her feet.*

MRS. FRANK, *she reads.*   "Here's an I.O.U. that I promise to pay. Ten hours of doing whatever you say. Signed, Anne Frank." *Mrs. Frank, touched, takes Anne in her arms, holding her close.*

DUSSEL, *to Anne.*   Ten hours of doing what you're told? *Anything* you're told?

ANNE.   That's right.

DUSSEL.   You wouldn't want to sell that, Mrs. Frank?

MRS. FRANK.   Never! This is the most precious gift I've ever had! *She sits, showing her present to the others. Anne hurries back to the satchel and pulls out a scarf, the scarf that Mr. Frank found in the first scene.*

ANNE, *offering it to her father.*   For Pim.

MR. FRANK.   Anneke . . . I wasn't supposed to have a present! *He takes it, unfolding it and showing it to the others.*

ANNE.   It's a muffler . . . to put round your neck . . . like an ascot, you know. I made it myself out of odds and ends . . . I knitted it in the dark each night, after I'd gone to bed. I'm afraid it looks better in the dark!

MR. FRANK, *putting it on.* It's fine. It fits me perfectly. Thank you, Annele. *Anne hands Peter a ball of paper, with a string attached to it.*

ANNE. That's for Mouschi.

PETER, *rising to bow.* On behalf of Mouschi, I thank you.

ANNE, *hesitant, handing him a gift.* And . . . this is yours . . . from Mrs. Quack Quack. *As he holds it gingerly in his hands.* Well . . . open it . . . Aren't you going to open it?

PETER. I'm scared to. I know something's going to jump out and hit me.

ANNE. No. It's nothing like that, really.

MRS. VAN DAAN, *as he is opening it.* What is it, Peter? Go on. Show it.

ANNE, *excitedly.* It's a safety razor!

DUSSEL. A what?

ANNE. A razor!

MRS. VAN DAAN, *looking at it.* You didn't make that out of odds and ends.

ANNE, *to Peter.* Miep got it for me. It's not new. It's second-hand. But you really do need a razor now.

DUSSEL. For what?

ANNE. Look on his upper lip . . . you can see the beginning of a moustache.

DUSSEL. He wants to get rid of that? Put a little milk on it and let the cat lick it off.

PETER, *starting for his room.* Think you're funny, don't you.

DUSSEL. Look! He can't wait. He's going in to try it!

PETER. I'm going to give Mouschi his present! *He goes into his room, slamming the door behind him.*

MR. VAN DAAN, *disgustedly.* Mouschi, Mouschi, Mouschi. *In the distance we hear a dog persistently barking. Anne brings a gift to Dussel.*

ANNE. And last but never least, my roommate, Mr. Dussel.

DUSSEL. For me? You have something for me? *He opens the small box she gives him.*

ANNE. I made them myself.

DUSSEL, *puzzled.* Capsules! Two capsules!

ANNE. They're ear-plugs!

DUSSEL. Ear-plugs?

ANNE. To put in your ears so you won't hear me when I thrash around at night. I saw them advertised in a magazine. They're not real ones . . . I made them out of cotton and candle wax. Try them . . . See if they don't work . . . see if you can hear me talk . . .

DUSSEL, *putting them in his ears.* Wait now until I get them in . . . so.

ANNE. Are you ready?

DUSSEL. Huh?

ANNE. Are you ready?

DUSSEL. Good God! They've gone inside! I can't get them out! *They laugh as Mr. Dussel jumps about, trying to shake the plugs out of his ears. Finally he gets them out. Putting them away.* Thank you, Anne! Thank you!

MR. VAN DAAN. A real Hanukkah!

MRS. VAN DAAN. Wasn't it cute of her?

MRS. FRANK. I don't know when she did it. *Together*

MARGOT. I love my present.

ANNE, *sitting at the table.* And now let's have the song, Father . . . please. . . . *To Dussel.* Have you heard the Hanukkah song, Mr. Dussel? The song is the whole thing! *She sings.* "Oh, Hanukkah! Oh Hanukkah! The sweet celebration . . ."

MR. FRANK, *quieting her.* I'm afraid, Anne, we shouldn't sing that song tonight. *To Dussel.* It's a song of jubilation, of rejoicing. One is apt to become too enthusiastic.

ANNE. Oh, please, please. Let's sing the song. I promise not to shout!

MR. FRANK. Very well. But quietly now . . . I'll keep an eye on you and when . . . *As Anne starts to sing, she is interrupted by Dussel, who is snorting and wheezing.*

DUSSEL, *pointing to Peter.* You . . . You! *Peter is coming from his bedroom, ostentatiously holding a bulge in his coat as if he were holding his cat, and dangling Anne's present before it.* How many times . . . I told you . . . Out! Out!

MR. VAN DAAN, *going to Peter.*   What's the matter with you?
Haven't you any sense? Get that cat out of here.

PETER, *innocently.*   Cat?

MR. VAN DAAN.   You heard me. Get it out of here!

PETER.   I have no cat.

*Delighted with his joke, he opens his coat and pulls out a bath
towel. The group at the table laugh, enjoying the joke.*

DUSSEL, *still wheezing.*   It doesn't need to be the cat . . . his
clothes are enough . . . when he comes out of that room . . .

MR. VAN DAAN.   Don't worry. You won't be bothered any
more. We're getting rid of it.

DUSSEL.   At last you listen to me. *He goes off into his bedroom.*

MR. VAN DAAN, *calling after him.*   I'm not doing it for you.
That's all in your mind . . . all of it! *He starts back to his place
at the table.* I'm doing it because I'm sick of seeing that cat
eat all our food.

PETER.   That's not true! I only give him bones . . . scraps . . .

MR. VAN DAAN.   Don't tell me! He gets fatter every day!
Damn cat looks better than any of us. Out he goes tonight!

PETER.   No! No!

ANNE.   Mr. van Daan, you can't do that! That's Peter's cat.
Peter loves that cat.

MRS. FRANK, *quietly.*   Anne.

PETER, *to Mr. van Daan.*   If he goes, I go.

MR. VAN DAAN.   Go! Go!

MRS. VAN DAAN.   You're not going and the cat's not going!
Now please . . . this is Hanukkah . . . Hanukkah . . . this is the
time to celebrate . . . What's the matter with all of you? Come
on, Anne. Let's have the song.

ANNE, *singing.*   "Oh, Hanukkah! Oh, Hanukkah!
                    The sweet celebration."

MR. FRANK, *rising.*   I think we should first blow out the candle . . . then we'll have something for tomorrow night.

MARGOT.   But, Father, you're supposed to let it burn itself
out.

MR. FRANK.   I'm sure that God understands shortages. *Before blowing it out.* "Praised be Thou, oh Lord our God, who hast sustained us and permitted us to celebrate this joyous festival."

He is about to blow out the candle when suddenly there is a crash of something falling below. They all freeze in horror, motionless. For a few seconds there is complete silence. Mr. Frank slips off his shoes. The others noiselessly follow his example. Mr. Frank turns out a light near him. He motions to Peter to turn off the centre lamp. Peter tries to reach it, realizes he cannot and gets up on a chair. Just as he is touching the lamp he loses his balance. The chair goes out from under him. He falls. The iron lamp shade crashes to the floor. There is a sound of feet below, running down the stairs.

MR. VAN DAAN, *under his breath.*   God Almighty! *The only light left comes from the Hanukkah candle. Dussel comes from his room. Mr. Frank creeps over to the stairwell and stands listening. The dog is heard barking excitedly.* Do you hear anything?

MR. FRANK, *in a whisper.*   No. I think they've gone.

MRS. VAN DAAN.   It's the Green Police. They've found us.

MR. FRANK.   If they had, they wouldn't have left. They'd be up here by now.

MRS. VAN DAAN.   I know it's the Green Police. They've gone to get help. That's all. They'll be back!

MR. VAN DAAN.   Or it may have been the Gestapo, looking for papers . . .

MR. FRANK, *interrupting.*   Or a thief, looking for money.

MRS. VAN DAAN.   We've got to do something . . . Quick! Quick! Before they come back.

MR. VAN DAAN.   There isn't anything to do. Just wait.

Mr. Frank holds up his hand for them to be quiet. He is listening intently. There is complete silence as they all strain to hear any sound from below. Suddenly Anne begins to sway. With a low cry she falls to the floor in a faint. Mrs. Frank goes to her quickly, sitting beside her on the floor and taking her in her arms.

MRS. FRANK.   Get some water, please! Get some water!

Margot starts for the sink.

◄───—   **I know it's the Green Police . . . They'll be back!**

MR. VAN DAAN, *grabbing Margot.*   No! No! No one's going to run water!

MR. FRANK.   If they've found us, they've found us. Get the water. *Margot starts again for the sink. Mr. Frank, getting a flashlight.* I'm going down.

Margot rushes to him, clinging to him. Anne struggles to consciousness.

MARGOT.   No, Father, no! There may be someone there, waiting . . . It may be a trap!

MR. FRANK.   This is Saturday. There is no way for us to know what has happened until Miep or Mr. Kraler comes on Monday morning. We cannot live with this uncertainty.

MARGOT.   Don't go, Father!

MRS. FRANK.   Hush, darling, hush. *Mr. Frank slips quietly out, down the steps and out through the door below.* Margot! Stay close to me.

Margot goes to her mother.

MR. VAN DAAN.   Shush! Shush!

Mrs. Frank whispers to Margot to get the water. Margot goes for it.

MRS. VAN DAAN.   Putti, where's our money? Get our money. I hear you can buy the Green Police off, so much a head. Go upstairs quick! Get the money!

MR. VAN DAAN.   Keep still!

MRS. VAN DAAN, *kneeling before him, pleading.*   Do you want to be dragged off to a concentration camp? Are you going to stand there and wait for them to come up and get you? Do something, I tell you!

MR. VAN DAAN, *pushing her aside.*   Will you keep still!

He goes over to the stairwell to listen. Peter goes to his mother, helping her up onto the sofa. There is a second of silence, then Anne can stand it no longer.

ANNE.   Someone go after Father! Make Father come back!

PETER, *starting for the door.*   I'll go.

MR. VAN DAAN.   Haven't you done enough?

He pushes Peter roughly away. In his anger against his father Peter grabs a chair as if to hit him with it, then puts it down, burying his face in his hands. Mrs. Frank begins to pray softly.

ANNE.   Please, please, Mr. van Daan. Get Father.

MR. VAN DAAN.   Quiet! Quiet!

Anne is shocked into silence. Mrs. Frank pulls her closer, holding her protectively in her arms.

MRS. FRANK, *softly, praying.*   "I lift up mine eyes unto the mountains, from whence cometh my help. My help cometh from the Lord who made heaven and earth. He will not suffer thy foot to be moved . . . He that keepeth thee will not slumber . . ."

She stops as she hears someone coming. They all watch the door tensely. Mr. Frank comes quietly in. Anne rushes to him, holding him tight.

MR. FRANK.   It was a thief. That noise must have scared him away.

MRS. VAN DAAN.   Thank God.

MR. FRANK.   He took the cash box. And the radio. He ran away in such a hurry that he didn't stop to shut the street door. It was swinging wide open. *A breath of relief sweeps over them.* I think it would be good to have some light.

MARGOT.   Are you sure it's all right?

MR. FRANK.   The danger has passed. *Margot goes to light the small lamp.* Don't be so terrified, Anne. We're safe.

DUSSEL.   Who says the danger has passed? Don't you realize we are in greater danger than ever?

MR. FRANK.   Mr. Dussel, will you be still!

Mr. Frank takes Anne back to the table, making her sit down with him, trying to calm her.

DUSSEL, *pointing to Peter.*   Thanks to this clumsy fool, there's someone now who knows we're up here! Someone now knows we're up here, hiding!

MRS. VAN DAAN, *going to Dussel.*   Someone knows we're here, yes. But who is the someone? A thief! A thief! You think a thief is going to go to the Green Police and say . . . I was rob-

"HANUKKAH"

YIDDISH FOLK SONG

ALLEGRO

OH HAN-UK-KAH OH HAN-UK-KAH THE SWEET CEL-E-BRA-TION A-

-ROUND THE FEAST WE GATH-ER IN COM-PLETE JUB-IL-A-TION

HAP-PI-EST OF SEA-SONS NOW IS_ HERE MAN-Y ARE THE REASONS

FOR GOOD CHEER TO-GETH-ER WE'LL WEATH-ER WHAT EV-ER TO-MOR-ROW MAY

BRING SO HEAR US RE-JOIC-ING AND MER-RI-LY VOIC-ING THE

HAN-UK-KAH SONG THAT WE SING HEY! SO HEAR US RE-JOIC-ING AND

MER-RI-LY VOIC-ING THE HAN-UK-KAH SONG THAT WE SING.

bing a place the other night and I heard a noise up over my head? You think a thief is going to do that?

DUSSEL. Yes. I think he will.

MRS. VAN DAAN, *hysterically.* You're crazy!
She stumbles back to her seat at the table. Peter follows protectively, pushing Dussel aside.

DUSSEL. I think some day he'll be caught and then he'll make a bargain with the Green Police . . . if they'll let him off, he'll tell them where some Jews are hiding!
He goes off into the bedroom. There is a second of appalled silence.

MR. VAN DAAN. He's right.

ANNE. Father, let's get out of here! We can't stay here now . . . Let's go . . .

MR. VAN DAAN. Go! Where?

MRS. FRANK, *sinking into her chair at the table.* Yes. Where?

MR. FRANK, *rising, to them all.* Have we lost all faith? All courage? A moment ago we thought that they'd come for us. We were sure it was the end. But it wasn't the end. We're alive, safe. *Mr. van Daan goes to the table and sits. Mr. Frank prays.* "We thank Thee, oh Lord our God, that in Thy infinite mercy Thou hast again seen fit to spare us." *He blows out the candle, then turns to Anne.* Come on, Anne. The song! Let's have the song! *He starts to sing. Anne finally starts falteringly to sing, as Mr. Frank urges her on. Her voice is hardly audible at first.*

ANNE, *singing.* "Oh, Hanukkah! Oh, Hanukkah!
The sweet . . . celebration . . ."

As she goes on singing, the others gradually join in, their voices still shaking with fear. Mrs. van Daan sobs as she sings.

GROUP. "Around the feast . . . we . . . gather
In complete . . . jubilation . . .
Happiest of sea . . . sons
Now is here.
Many are the reasons for good cheer."

Dussel comes from the bedroom. He comes over to the table, standing beside Margot, listening to them as they sing.

"Together
We'll weather
Whatever tomorrow may bring."

As they sing on with growing courage, the lights start to dim.

"So hear us rejoicing
And merrily voicing
The Hanukkah song that we sing.
Hoy!"

The lights are out. The curtain starts slowly to fall.

"Hear us rejoicing
And merrily voicing
The Hanukkah song that we sing."

They are still singing, as the curtain falls.

Curtain

ACT TWO

SCENE 1

In the darkness we hear Anne's voice, again reading from the diary.

ANNE'S VOICE. Saturday, the first of January, nineteen forty-four. Another new year has begun and we find ourselves still in our hiding place. We have been here now for one year, five months and twenty-five days. It seems that our life is at a standstill.

The curtain rises on the scene. It is late afternoon. Everyone is bundled up against the cold. In the main room Mrs. Frank is taking down the laundry which is hung across the back. Mr. Frank sits in the chair down left, reading. Margot is lying on the couch with a blanket over her and the many-coloured knitted scarf around her throat. Anne is seated at the centre table, writing in her diary. Peter, Mr. and Mrs. van Daan and Dussel are all in their own rooms, reading or lying down.

As the lights dim on, Anne's voice continues, without a break.

ANNE'S VOICE. We are all a little thinner. The van Daans' "discussions" are as violent as ever. Mother still does not understand me. But then I don't understand her either. There is one great change, however. A change in myself. I read somewhere that girls of my age don't feel quite certain of themselves. That they become quiet within and begin to think of the miracle that is taking place in their bodies. I think that what is happening to me is so wonderful . . . not only what can be seen, but what is taking place inside. I have a feeling that I have a sweet secret. *We hear the chimes and then a hymn being played on the carillon outside.*

The buzzer of the door below suddenly sounds. Everyone is startled, Mr. Frank tiptoes cautiously to the top of the steps and listens. Again the buzzer sounds, in Miep's V-for-Victory signal.

MR. FRANK.   It's Miep!

*He goes quickly down the steps to unbolt the door. Mrs. Frank
calls upstairs to the van Daans and then to Peter.*

MRS. FRANK.   Wake up, everyone! Miep is here! *Anne quickly puts her diary away. Margot sits up, pulling the blanket
around her shoulders. Mr. Dussel sits on the edge of the bed,
listening, disgruntled. Miep comes up the steps, followed by
Mr. Kraler. They bring flowers, books, newspapers, etc. Anne
rushes to Miep, throwing her arms affectionately around her.*
Miep . . . *and* Mr. Kraler . . . What a delightful surprise!

MR. KRALER.   We came to bring you New Year's greetings.

MRS. FRANK.   You shouldn't . . . you should have at least one
day to yourselves.

*She goes quickly to the stove and brings down teacups and
tea for all of them.*

ANNE.   Don't say that, it's so wonderful to see them! *Sniffing
at Miep's coat.* I can smell the wind and the cold on your
clothes.

MIEP, *giving her the flowers.*   There you are. *Then to Margot, feeling her forehead.* How are you, Margot? . . . Feeling
any better?

MARGOT.   I'm all right.

ANNE.   We filled her full of every kind of pill so she won't
cough and make a noise.

*She runs into her room to put the flowers in water. Mr. and
Mrs. van Daan come from upstairs. Outside there is the sound
of a band playing.*

MRS. VAN DAAN.   Well, hello, Miep. Mr. Kraler.

MR. KRALER, *giving a bouquet of flowers to Mrs. van Daan.*
With my hope for peace in the New Year.

PETER, *anxiously.*   Miep, have you seen Mouschi? Have you
seen him anywhere around?

MIEP.   I'm sorry, Peter. I asked everyone in the neighbourhood had they seen a grey cat. But they said no.

*Mrs. Frank gives Miep a cup of tea. Mr. Frank comes up the
steps, carrying a small cake on a plate.*

MR. FRANK. Look what Miep's brought for us!

MRS. FRANK, *taking it.* A cake!

MR. VAN DAAN. A cake! *He pinches Miep's cheeks gaily and hurries up to the cupboard.* I'll get some plates.

Dussel, in his room, hastily puts a coat on and starts out to join the others.

MRS. FRANK. Thank you, Miepia. You shouldn't have done it. You must have used all of your sugar ration for weeks. *Giving it to Mrs. van Daan.* It's beautiful, isn't it?

MRS. VAN DAAN. It's been ages since I even saw a cake. Not since you brought us one last year. *Without looking at the cake, to Miep.* Remember? Don't you remember, you gave us one on New Year's Day? Just this time last year? I'll never forget it because you had "Peace in nineteen forty-three" on it. *She looks at the cake and reads.* "Peace in nineteen forty-four!"

MIEP. Well, it has to come sometime, you know. *As Dussel comes from his room.* Hello, Mr. Dussel.

MR. KRALER. How are you?

MR. VAN DAAN, *bringing plates and a knife.* Here's the knife, *liefje.* Now, how many of us are there?

MIEP. None for me, thank you.

MR. FRANK. Oh, please. You must.

MIEP. I couldn't.

MR. VAN DAAN. Good! That leaves one . . . two . . . three . . . seven of us.

DUSSEL Eight! Eight! It's the same number as it always is!

MR. VAN DAAN. I left Margot out. I take it for granted Margot won't eat any.

ANNE. Why wouldn't she!

MRS. FRANK. I think it won't harm her.

MR. VAN DAAN. All right! All right! I just didn't want her to start coughing again, that's all.

DUSSEL. And please, Mrs. Frank should cut the cake.

MR. VAN DAAN. What's the difference? ⎫

MRS. VAN DAAN. It's not Mrs. Frank's cake, ⎬ *Together*
is it, Miep? It's for all of us. ⎭

DUSSEL.   Mrs. Frank divides things better.

MRS. VAN DAAN, *going to Dussel.*   What are ⎫
you trying to say?   ⎪
MR. VAN DAAN.   Oh, come on! Stop wasting ⎬ *Together*
time!   ⎭

MRS. VAN DAAN, *to Dussel.*   Don't I always give everybody exactly the same? Don't I?

MR. VAN DAAN.   Forget it, Kerli.

MRS. VAN DAAN.   No. I want an answer! Don't I?

DUSSEL.   Yes. Yes. Everybody gets exactly the same . . . except Mr. van Daan always gets a little bit more.

Van Daan advances on Dussel, the knife still in his hand.

MR. VAN DAAN.   That's a lie!

Dussel retreats before the onslaught of the van Daans.

MR. FRANK.   Please, please! *Then to Miep.* You see what a little sugar cake does to us? It goes right to our heads!

MR. VAN DAAN, *handing Mrs. Frank the knife.*   Here you are, Mrs. Frank.

MRS. FRANK.   Thank you. *Then to Miep as she goes to the table to cut the cake.* Are you sure you won't have some?

MIEP, *drinking her tea.*   No, really, I have to go in a minute. *The sound of the band fades out in the distance.*

PETER, *to Miep.*   Maybe Mouschi went back to our house . . . they say that cats . . . Do you ever get over there . . . ? I mean . . . do you suppose you could . . . ?

MIEP.   I'll try, Peter. The first minute I get I'll try. But I'm afraid, with him gone a week . . .

DUSSEL.   Make up your mind, already someone has had a nice big dinner from that cat!

Peter is furious, inarticulate. He starts toward Dussel as if to hit him. Mr. Frank stops him. Mrs. Frank speaks quickly to ease the situation.

MRS. FRANK, *to Miep.*   This is delicious, Miep!

MRS. VAN DAAN, *eating hers.*   Delicious!

MR. VAN DAAN, *finishing it in one gulp.*   Dirk's in luck to get a girl who can bake like this!

MIEP, *putting down her empty teacup.* I have to run. Dirk's taking me to a party tonight.

ANNE. How heavenly! Remember now what everyone is wearing, and what you have to eat and everything, so you can tell us tomorrow.

MIEP. I'll give you a full report! Good-bye, everyone!

MR. VAN DAAN, *to Miep.* Just a minute. There's something I'd like you to do for me.

He hurries off up the stairs to his room.

MRS. VAN DAAN, *sharply.* Putti, where are you going? *She rushes up the stairs after him, calling hysterically.* What do you want? Putti, what are you going to do?

MIEP, *to Peter.* What's wrong?

PETER, *his sympathy is with his mother.* Father says he's going to sell her fur coat. She's crazy about that old fur coat.

DUSSEL. Is it possible? Is it possible that anyone is so silly as to worry about a fur coat in times like this?

PETER. It's none of your darn business . . . and if you say one more thing . . . I'll, I'll take you and I'll . . . I mean it . . . I'll . . .

There is a piercing scream from Mrs. van Daan above. She grabs at the fur coat as Mr. van Daan is starting downstairs with it.

MRS. VAN DAAN. No! No! No! Don't you dare take that! You hear? It's mine! *Downstairs Peter turns away, embarrassed, miserable.* My father gave me that! You didn't give it to me. You have no right. Let go of it . . . you hear?

Mr. van Daan pulls the coat from her hands and hurries downstairs. Mrs. van Daan sinks to the floor, sobbing. As Mr. van Daan comes into the main room the others look away, embarrassed for him.

MR. VAN DAAN, *to Mr. Kraler.* Just a little—discussion over the advisability of selling this coat. As I have often reminded Mrs. van Daan, it's very selfish of her to keep it when people outside are in such desperate need of clothing . . . *He gives the coat to Miep.* So if you will please to sell it for us? It should fetch a good price. And by the way, will you get me cigarettes. I don't care what kind they are . . . get all you can.

MIEP.   It's terribly difficult to get them, Mr. van Daan. But I'll try. Good-bye.

She goes. Mr. Frank follows her down the steps to bolt the door after her. Mrs. Frank gives Mr. Kraler a cup of tea.

MRS. FRANK.   Are you sure you won't have some cake, Mr. Kraler?

MR. KRALER.   I'd better not.

MR. VAN DAAN.   You're still feeling badly? What does your doctor say?

MR. KRALER.   I haven't been to him.

MRS. FRANK.   Now, Mr. Kraler! . . .

MR. KRALER, *sitting at the table.*   Oh, I tried. But you can't get near a doctor these days . . . they're so busy. After weeks I finally managed to get one on the telephone. I told him I'd like an appointment . . . I wasn't feeling very well. You know what he answers . . . over the telephone . . . Stick out your tongue! *They laugh. He turns to Mr. Frank as Mr. Frank comes back.* I have some contracts here . . . I wonder if you'd look over them with me . . .

MR. FRANK, *putting out his hand.*   Of course.

MR. KRALER, *he rises.*   If we could go downstairs . . . *Mr. Frank starts ahead, Mr. Kraler speaks to the others.* Will you forgive us? I won't keep him but a minute.

He starts to follow Mr. Frank down the steps.

MARGOT, *with sudden foreboding.*   What's happened? Something's happened! Hasn't it, Mr. Kraler?

Mr. Kraler stops and comes back, trying to reassure Margot with a pretence of casualness.

MR. KRALER.   No, really. I want your father's advice . . .

MARGOT.   Something's gone wrong! I know it!

MR. FRANK, *coming back, to Mr. Kraler.*   If it's something that concerns us here, it's better that we all hear it.

MR. KRALER, *turning to him, quietly.*   But . . . the children . . ?

MR. FRANK.   What they'd imagine would be worse than any reality.

As Mr. Kraler speaks, they all listen with intense apprehension. Mrs. van Daan comes down the stairs and sits on the bottom step.

MR. KRALER.   It's a man in the storeroom . . . I don't know whether or not you remember him . . [Carl] about fifty, heavyset, near-sighted . . . He came with us just before you left.

MR. FRANK.   He was from [Utrecht?]

MR. KRALER.   That's the man. A couple of weeks ago, when I was in the storeroom, he closed the door and asked me . . . how's Mr. Frank? What do you hear from Mr. Frank? I told him I only knew there was a rumour that you were in Switzerland. He said he'd heard that rumour too, but he thought I might know something more. I didn't pay any attention to it . . . but then a thing happened yesterday . . . He'd brought some invoices to the office for me to sign. As I was going through them, I looked up. He was standing staring at the bookcase . . . your bookcase. He said he thought he remembered a door there . . . Wasn't there a door there that used to go up to the loft? Then he told me he wanted more money. Twenty guilders more a week.

MR. VAN DAAN.   Blackmail!

MR. FRANK.   Twenty guilders? Very modest blackmail.

MR. VAN DAAN.   That's just the beginning.

DUSSEL, *coming to Mr. Frank.*   You know what I think? He was the thief who was down there that night. That's how he knows we're here.

MR. FRANK, *to Mr. Kraler.*   How was it left? What did you tell him?

MR. KRALER.   I said I had to think about it. What shall I do? Pay him the money? . . . Take a chance on firing him . . . or what? I don't know.

DUSSEL, *frantic.*   For God's sake don't fire him! Pay him what he asks . . . keep him here where you can have your eye on him.

MR. FRANK.   Is it so much that he's asking? What are they paying nowadays?

MR. KRALER.   He could get it in a war plant. But this isn't a war plant. Mind you, I don't know if he really knows . . . or if he doesn't know.

MR. FRANK.   Offer him half. Then we'll soon find out if it's blackmail or not.

DUSSEL.   And if it is? We've got to pay it, haven't we? Anything he asks we've got to pay!

MR. FRANK.   Let's decide that when the time comes.

MR. KRALER.   This may be all my imagination. You get to a point, these days, where you suspect everyone and everything. Again and again . . . on some simple look or word, I've found myself . . .

The telephone rings in the office below.

MRS. VAN DAAN, *hurrying to Mr. Kraler.*   There's the telephone! What does that mean, the telephone ringing on a holiday?

MR. KRALER.   That's my wife. I told her I had to go over some papers in my office . . . to call me there when she got out of church. *He starts out.* I'll offer him half then. Goodbye . . . we'll hope for the best!

The group call their good-byes half-heartedly. Mr. Frank follows Mr. Kraler, to bolt the door below. During the following scene, Mr. Frank comes back up and stands listening, disturbed.

DUSSEL, *to Mr. van Daan.*   You can thank your son for this . . . smashing the light! I tell you, it's just a question of time now.

He goes to the window at the back and stands looking out.

MARGOT.   Sometimes I wish the end would come . . . whatever it is.

MRS. FRANK, *shocked.*   Margot!

Anne goes to Margot, sitting beside her on the couch with her arms around her.

MARGOT.   Then at least we'd know where we were.

MRS. FRANK.   You should be ashamed of yourself! Talking that way! Think how lucky we are! Think of the thousands dying in the war, every day. Think of the people in concentration camps.

ANNE, *interrupting.* What's the good of that? What's the good of thinking of misery when you're already miserable? That's stupid!

MRS. FRANK. Anne!

As Anne goes on raging at her mother, Mrs. Frank tries to break in, in an effort to quiet her.

ANNE. We're young, Margot and Peter and I! You grown-ups have had your chance! But look at us . . . If we begin thinking of all the horror in the world, we're lost! We're trying to hold onto some kind of ideals . . . when everything . . . ideals, hopes . . . everything, are being destroyed! It isn't our fault that the world is in such a mess! We weren't around when all this started! So don't try to take it out on us!

She rushes off to her room, slamming the door after her. She picks up a brush from the chest and hurls it to the floor. Then she sits on the settee, trying to control her anger.

MR. VAN DAAN. She talks as if we started the war! Did we start the war?

He spots Anne's cake. As he starts to take it, Peter anticipates him.

PETER. She left her cake. *He starts for Anne's room with the cake. There is silence in the main room. Mrs. van Daan goes up to her room, followed by van Daan. Dussel stays looking out the window. Mr. Frank brings Mrs. Frank her cake. She eats it slowly, without relish. Mr. Frank takes his cake to Margot and sits quietly on the sofa beside her. Peter stands in the doorway of Anne's darkened room, looking at her, then makes a little movement to let her know he is there. Anne sits up, quickly, trying to hide the signs of her tears. Peter holds out the cake to her.* You left this.

ANNE, *dully.* Thanks.

Peter starts to go out, then comes back.

PETER. I thought you were fine just now. You know just how to talk to them. You know just how to say it. I'm no good . . .

I never can think . . . especially when I'm mad . . . That Dussel . . . when he said that about Mouschi . . . someone eating him . . . all I could think is . . . I wanted to hit him. I wanted to give him such a . . . a . . . that he'd . . . That's what I used to do when there was an argument at school . . . That's the way I . . . but here . . . And an old man like that . . . it wouldn't be so good.

ANNE. You're making a big mistake about me. I do it all wrong. I say too much. I go too far. I hurt people's feelings . . .

Dussel leaves the window, going to his room.

PETER. I think you're just fine . . . What I want to say . . . if it wasn't for you around here, I don't know. What I mean . . .

Peter is interrupted by Dussel's turning on the light. Dussel stands in the doorway, startled to see Peter. Peter advances toward him forbiddingly. Dussel backs out of the room. Peter closes the door on him.

ANNE. Do you mean it, Peter? Do you really mean it?

PETER. I said it, didn't I?

ANNE. Thank you, Peter!

In the main room Mr. and Mrs. Frank collect the dishes and take them to the sink, washing them. Margot lies down again on the couch. Dussel, lost, wanders into Peter's room and takes up a book, starting to read.

PETER, *looking at the photographs on the wall.* You've got quite a collection.

ANNE. Wouldn't you like some in your room? I could give you some. Heaven knows you spend enough time in there . . . doing heaven knows what . . .

PETER. It's easier. A fight starts, or an argument . . . I duck in there.

ANNE. You're lucky, having a room to go to. His lordship is always here . . . I hardly ever get a minute alone. When they start in on me, I can't duck away. I have to stand there and take it.

PETER. You gave some of it back just now.

ANNE. I get so mad. They've formed their opinions . . . about everything . . . but we . . . we're still trying to find out . . . We have problems here that no other people our age have ever had. And just as you think you've solved them, something comes along and bang! You have to start all over again.

PETER.   At least you've got someone you can talk to.

ANNE.   Not really. Mother . . . I never discuss anything serious with her. She doesn't understand. Father's all right. We can talk about everything . . . everything but one thing. Mother. He simply won't talk about her. I don't think you can be really intimate with anyone if he holds something back, do you?

PETER.   I think your father's fine.

ANNE.   Oh, he is, Peter! He is! He's the only one who's ever given me the feeling that I have any sense. But anyway, nothing can take the place of school and play and friends of your own age . . . or near your age . . . can it?

PETER.   I suppose you miss your friends and all.

ANNE.   It isn't just . . . *She breaks off, staring up at him for a second.* Isn't it funny, you and I? Here we've been seeing each other every minute for almost a year and a half, and this is the first time we've ever really talked. It helps a lot to have someone to talk to, don't you think? It helps you to let off steam.

PETER, *going to the door.*   Well, any time you want to let off steam, you can come into my room.

ANNE, *following him.*   I can get up an awful lot of steam. You'll have to be careful how you say that.

PETER.   It's all right with me.

ANNE.   Do you mean it?

PETER.   I said it, didn't I?

He goes out. Anne stands in her doorway looking after him. As Peter gets to his door he stands for a minute looking back at her. Then he goes into his room. Dussel rises as he comes in, and quickly passes him, going out. He starts across for his room. Anne sees him coming, and pulls her door shut. Dussel turns back toward Peter's room. Peter pulls his door shut. Dussel stands there, bewildered, forlorn.
The scene slowly dims out. The curtain falls on the scene.

*Anne's voice comes over in the darkness . . . faintly at first,
and then with growing strength.*

ANNE'S VOICE. We've had bad news. The people from whom
Miep got our ration books have been arrested. So we have had
to cut down on our food. Our stomachs are so empty that they
rumble and make strange noises, all in different keys. Mr.
van Daan's is deep and low, like a bass fiddle. Mine is high,
whistling like a flute. As we all sit around waiting for supper,
it's like an orchestra tuning up. It only needs Toscanini to
raise his baton and we'd be off in the Ride of the Valkyries.
Monday, the sixth of March, nineteen forty-four. Mr. Kraler is
in the hospital. It seems he has ulcers. Pim says we are his
ulcers. Miep has to run the business and us too. The Americans
have landed on the southern tip of Italy. Father looks for a
quick finish to the war. Mr. Dussel is waiting every day for
the warehouse man to demand more money. Have I been
skipping too much from one subject to another? I can't help
it. I feel that spring is coming. I feel it in my whole body and
soul. I feel utterly confused. I am longing . . . so longing . . .
for everything . . . for friends . . . for someone to talk to . . .
someone who understands . . . someone young, who feels as
I do . . .

*As these last lines are being said, the curtain rises on the scene.
The lights dim on. Anne's voice fades out.*

SCENE 2

*It is evening, after supper. From outside we hear the sound of
children playing. The "grownups," with the exception of Mr.
van Daan, are all in the main room. Mrs. Frank is doing some
mending, Mrs. van Daan is reading a fashion magazine. Mr.
Frank is going over business accounts. Dussel, in his dentist's
jacket, is pacing up and down, impatient to get into his bedroom. Mr. van Daan is upstairs working on a piece of embroidery in an embroidery frame.*

In his room Peter is sitting before the mirror, smoothing his hair. As the scene goes on, he puts on his tie, brushes his coat and puts it on, preparing himself meticulously for a visit from Anne. On his wall are now hung some of Anne's motion picture stars.

In her room Anne too is getting dressed. She stands before the mirror in her slip, trying various ways of dressing her hair. Margot is seated on the sofa, hemming a skirt for Anne to wear.

In the main room Dussel can stand it no longer. He comes over, rapping sharply on the door of his and Anne's bedroom.

ANNE, *calling to him.* No, no, Mr. Dussel! I am not dressed yet. *Dussel walks away, furious, sitting down and burying his head in his hands. Anne turns to Margot.* How is that? How does that look?

MARGOT, *glancing at her briefly.* Fine.

ANNE. You didn't even look.

MARGOT. Of course I did. It's fine.

ANNE. Margot, tell me, am I terribly ugly?

MARGOT. Oh, stop fishing.

ANNE. No. No. Tell me.

MARGOT. Of course you're not. You've got nice eyes . . . and a lot of animation, and . . .

ANNE A little vague, aren't you?

Outside, Mrs. Frank, feeling sorry for Dussel, comes over, knocking at the girls' door.

MRS. FRANK, *outside.* May I come in?

MARGOT. Come in, Mother.

MRS. FRANK, *shutting the door behind her.* Mr. Dussel's impatient to get in here.

ANNE. Heavens, he takes the room for himself the entire day.

MRS. FRANK, *gently.* Anne, dear, you're not going in again tonight to see Peter?

ANNE, *dignified.* That is my intention.

MRS. FRANK. But you've already spent a great deal of time in there today.

ANNE.   I was in there exactly twice. Once to get the diction-ary, and then three-quarters of an hour before supper.

MRS. FRANK.   Aren't you afraid you're disturbing him?

ANNE.   Mother, I have some intuition.

MRS. FRANK.   Then may I ask you this much, Anne. Please don't shut the door when you go in.

ANNE.   You sound like Mrs. van Daan!

She picks up her blouse, putting it on.

MRS. FRANK.   No. No. I don't mean to suggest anything wrong. I only wish that you wouldn't expose yourself to criti-cism . . . that you wouldn't give Mrs. van Daan the oppor-tunity to be unpleasant.

ANNE.   Mrs. van Daan doesn't need an opportunity to be unpleasant!

MRS. FRANK.   Everyone's on edge, worried about Mr. Kraler. This is one more thing . . .

ANNE.   I'm sorry, Mother. I'm going to Peter's room. I'm not going to let Petronella van Daan spoil our friendship.

Mrs. Frank hesitates for a second, then goes out, closing the door after her. She gets a pack of playing cards and sits at the centre table, playing solitaire. In Anne's room Margot hands the finished skirt to Anne. As Anne is putting it on, Margot takes off her high-heeled shoes and stuffs paper in the toes so that Anne can wear them.

MARGOT, *to Anne.*   Why don't you two talk in the main room? It'd save a lot of trouble. It's hard on Mother, having to listen to those remarks from Mrs. van Daan and not say a word.

ANNE.   Why doesn't she say a word? I think it's ridiculous to take it and take it.

MARGOT.   You don't understand Mother at all, do you? She can't talk back. She's not like you. It's just not in her nature to fight back.

ANNE.   Anyway . . . the only one I worry about is you. I feel awfully guilty about you.

She sits on the stool near Margot, putting on Margot's high-heeled shoes.

MARGOT.   What about?

ANNE.   I mean, every time I go into Peter's room, I have a feeling I may be hurting you. *Margot shakes her head.* I know if it were me, I'd be wild. I'd be desperately jealous, if it were me.

MARGOT.   Well, I'm not.

ANNE.   You don't feel badly? Really? Truly? You're not jealous?

MARGOT.   Of course I'm jealous . . . jealous that you've got something to get up in the morning for . . . But jealous of you and Peter? No.

Anne goes back to the mirror.

ANNE.   Maybe there's nothing to be jealous of. Maybe he doesn't really like me. Maybe I'm just taking the place of his cat . . . *She picks up a pair of short white gloves, putting them on.* Wouldn't you like to come in with us?

MARGOT.   I have a book.

The sound of the children playing outside fades out. In the main room Dussel can stand it no longer. He jumps up, going to the bedroom door and knocking sharply.

DUSSEL.   Will you please let me in my room!

ANNE.   Just a minute, dear, dear Mr. Dussel. *She picks up her mother's pink stole and adjusts it elegantly over her shoulders, then gives a last look in the mirror.* Well, here I go . . . to run the gauntlet.

She starts out, followed by Margot.

DUSSEL, *as she appears—sarcastic.* Thank you so much.

Dussel goes into his room. Anne goes toward Peter's room, passing Mrs. van Daan and her parents at the centre table.

MRS. VAN DAAN.   My God, look at her! *Anne pays no attention. She knocks at Peter's door.* I don't know what good it is to have a son. I never see him. He wouldn't care if I killed myself. *Peter opens the door and stands aside for Anne to come in.* Just a minute, Anne. *She goes to them at the door.* I'd like to say a few words to my son. Do you mind? *Peter and Anne stand waiting.* Peter, I don't want you staying up till all hours

tonight. You've got to have your sleep. You're a growing boy.
You hear?

MRS. FRANK.   Anne won't stay late. She's going to bed prompt-
ly at nine. Aren't you, Anne?

ANNE.   Yes, Mother . . . *To Mrs. van Daan.* May we go now?

MRS. VAN DAAN.   Are you asking me? I didn't know I had
anything to say about it.

MRS. FRANK.   Listen for the chimes, Anne dear.

*The two young people go off into Peter's room, shutting the
door after them.*

MRS. VAN DAAN, *to Mrs. Frank.*   In my day it was the boys
who called on the girls. Not the girls on the boys.

MRS. FRANK.   You know how young people like to feel that
they have secrets. Peter's room is the only place where they
can talk.

MRS. VAN DAAN.   Talk! That's not what they called it when
I was young.

*Mrs. van Daan goes off to the bathroom. Margot settles down
to read her book. Mr. Frank puts his papers away and brings
a chess game to the centre table. He and Mrs. Frank start to
play. In Peter's room, Anne speaks to Peter, indignant, humiliated.*

ANNE.   Aren't they awful? Aren't they impossible? Treating
us as if we were still in the nursery.

She sits on the cot. Peter gets a bottle of pop and two glasses.

PETER.   Don't let it bother you. It doesn't bother me.

ANNE.   I suppose you can't really blame them . . . they think
back to what *they* were like at our age. They don't realize
how much more advanced we are . . . When you think what
wonderful discussions we've had! . . . Oh, I forgot. I was going
to bring you some more pictures.

PETER.   Oh, these are fine, thanks.

ANNE.   Don't you want some more? Miep just brought me
some new ones.

PETER.   Maybe later.

*He gives her a glass of pop and, taking some for himself, sits
down facing her.*

ANNE, *looking up at one of the photographs.* I remember
when I got that . . . I won it. I bet Jopie that I could eat five
ice-cream cones. We'd all been playing ping-pong . . . We
used to have heavenly times . . . we'd finish up with ice cream
at the Delphi, or the Oasis, where Jews were allowed . . . there'd
always be a lot of boys . . . we'd laugh and joke . . . I'd like to
go back to it for a few days or a week. But after that I know I'd
be bored to death. I think more seriously about life now. I
want to be a journalist . . . or something. I love to write. What
do you want to do?

PETER. I thought I might go off some place . . . work on a
farm or something . . . some job that doesn't take much brains.

ANNE. You shouldn't talk that way. You've got the most
awful inferiority complex.

PETER. I know I'm not smart.

ANNE. That isn't true. You're much better than I am in
dozens of things . . . arithmetic and algebra and . . . well, you're
a million times better than I am in algebra. *With sudden
directness.* You like Margot, don't you? Right from the start
you liked her, liked her much better than me.

PETER, *uncomfortably.* Oh, I don't know.

*In the main room Mrs. van Daan comes from the bathroom
and goes over to the sink, polishing a coffee pot.*

ANNE. It's all right. Everyone feels that way. Margot's so
good. She's sweet and bright and beautiful and I'm not.

PETER. I wouldn't say that.

ANNE. Oh, no, I'm not. I know that. I know quite well that
I'm not a beauty. I never have been and never shall be.

PETER. I don't agree at all. I think you're pretty.

ANNE. That's not true!

PETER. And another thing. You've changed . . . from at first,
I mean.

ANNE. I have?

PETER. I used to think you were awful noisy.

ANNE.   And what do you think now, Peter? How have I changed?

PETER.   Well . . . er . . . you're . . . quieter.

In his room Dussel takes his pyjamas and toilet articles and goes into the bathroom to change.

ANNE.   I'm glad you don't just hate me.

PETER.   I never said that.

ANNE.   I bet when you get out of here you'll never think of me again.

PETER.   That's crazy.

ANNE.   When you get back with all your friends, you're going to say . . . now what did I ever see in that Mrs. Quack Quack.

PETER.   I haven't got any friends.

ANNE.   Oh, Peter, of course you have. Everyone has friends.

PETER.   Not me. I don't want any. I get along all right without them.

ANNE.   Does that mean you can get along without me? I think of myself as your friend.

PETER.   No. If they were all like you, it'd be different.

He takes the glasses and the bottle and puts them away. There is a second's silence and then Anne speaks, hesitantly, shyly.

ANNE.   Peter, did you ever kiss a girl?

PETER.   Yes. Once.

ANNE, *to cover her feelings.*   That picture's crooked. *Peter goes over, straightening the photograph.* Was she pretty?

PETER.   Huh?

ANNE.   The girl that you kissed.

PETER.   I don't know. I was blindfolded. *He comes back and sits down again.*   It was at a party. One of those kissing games.

ANNE, *relieved.*   Oh. I don't suppose that really counts, does it?

PETER.   It didn't with me.

ANNE.   I've been kissed twice. Once a man I'd never seen before kissed me on the cheek when he picked me up off the ice and I was crying. And the other was Mr. Koophuis, a friend of Father's who kissed my hand. You wouldn't say those counted, would you?

PETER. I wouldn't say so.

ANNE. I know almost for certain that Margot would never kiss anyone unless she was engaged to them. And I'm sure too that Mother never touched a man before Pim. But I don't know . . . things are so different now . . . What do you think? Do you think a girl shouldn't kiss anyone except if she's engaged or something? It's so hard to try to think what to do, when here we are with the whole world falling around our ears and you think . . . well . . . you don't know what's going to happen tomorrow and . . . What do you think?

PETER. I suppose it'd depend on the girl. Some girls, anything they do's wrong. But others . . . well . . . it wouldn't necessarily be wrong with them. *The carillon starts to strike nine o'clock.* I've always thought that when two people . . .

ANNE. Nine o'clock. I have to go.

PETER. That's right.

ANNE, *without moving.* Good night.

There is a second's pause, then Peter gets up and moves toward the door.

PETER. You won't let them stop you coming?

ANNE. No. *She rises and starts for the door.* Sometime I might bring my diary. There are so many things in it that I want to talk over with you. There's a lot about you.

PETER. What kind of thing?

ANNE. I wouldn't want you to see some of it. I thought you were a nothing, just the way you thought about me.

PETER. Did you change your mind, the way I changed my mind about you?

ANNE. Well . . . You'll see . . .

For a second Anne stands looking up at Peter, longing for him to kiss her. As he makes no move she turns away. Then suddenly Peter grabs her awkwardly in his arms, kissing her on the cheek. Anne walks out dazed. She stands for a minute, her back to the people in the main room. As she regains her poise she goes to her mother and father and Margot, silently kissing them. They murmur their good nights to her. As she is about to open her bedroom door, she catches sight of Mrs. van Daan. She goes quickly to her, taking her face in her hands and kissing her first on one cheek and then on the other. Then she hurries off into her room. Mrs. van Daan looks after her, and then looks over at Peter's room. Her suspicions are confirmed.

MRS. VAN DAAN.   Ah hah!

The lights dim out. The curtain falls on the scene. In the darkness Anne's voice comes faintly at first and then with growing strength.

ANNE'S VOICE.   By this time we all know each other so well that if anyone starts to tell a story, the rest can finish it for him. We're having to cut down still further on our meals. What makes it worse, the rats have been at work again. They've carried off some of our precious food. Even Mr. Dussel wishes now that Mouschi was here. Thursday, the twentieth of April, nineteen forty-four. Invasion fever is mounting every day. Miep tells us that people outside talk of nothing else. For myself, life has become much more pleasant. I often go to Peter's room after supper. Oh, don't think I'm in love, because I'm not. But it does make life more bearable to have someone with whom you can exchange views. No more tonight. P.S. . . . I must be honest. I must confess that I actually live for the next meeting. Is there anything lovelier than to sit under the skylight and feel the sun on your cheeks and have a darling boy by your side? I admit now that I'm glad the van Daans had a son and not a daughter. I've outgrown another dress. That's the third. I'm having to wear Margot's clothes after all. I'm working hard on my French and am now reading *La Belle Nivernaise.*

As she is saying the last lines—the curtain rises on the scene. The lights dim on, as Anne's voice fades out.

SCENE 3

*It is night, a few weeks later. Everyone is in bed. There is
complete quiet. In the van Daans' room a match flares up for
a moment and then is quickly put out. Mr. van Daan, in bare
feet, dressed in underwear and trousers, is dimly seen coming
stealthily down the stairs and into the main room, where Mr.
and Mrs. Frank and Margot are sleeping. He goes to the food
safe and again lights a match. Then he cautiously opens the
safe, taking out a half-loaf of bread. As he closes the safe, it
creaks. He stands rigid. Mrs. Frank sits up in bed. She sees him.*

MRS. FRANK, *screaming.*   Otto! Otto! *Komme schnell!*

The rest of the people wake, hurriedly getting up.

MR. FRANK.   *Was ist los? Was ist passiert?*

Dussel, followed by Anne, comes from his room.

MRS. FRANK, *as she rushes over to Mr. van Daan.   Er stiehlt
das Essen!*

DUSSEL, *grabbing Mr. van Daan.*   You! You! Give me that.

MRS. VAN DAAN, *coming down the stairs.*   Putti . . . Putti . . .
what is it?

DUSSEL, *his hands on van Daan's neck.*   You dirty thief . . .
stealing food . . . you good-for-nothing . . .

MR. FRANK.   Mr. Dussel! For God's sake! Help me, Peter!

*Peter comes over, trying, with Mr. Frank, to separate the two
struggling men.*

PETER.   Let him go! Let go!

*Dussel drops Mr. van Daan, pushing him away. He shows them
the end of a loaf of bread that he has taken from van Daan.*

DUSSEL.   You greedy, selfish . . . !

Margot turns on the lights.

MRS. VAN DAAN.   Putti . . . what is it?

*All of Mrs. Frank's gentleness, her self-control, is gone. She is
outraged, in a frenzy of indignation.*

MRS. FRANK.   The bread! He was stealing the bread!

DUSSEL.   It was you, and all the time we thought it was the rats!

MR. FRANK.   Mr. van Daan, how could you!

MR. VAN DAAN.   I'm hungry.

MRS. FRANK.   We're all of us hungry! I see the children getting thinner and thinner. Your own son Peter . . . I've heard him moan in his sleep, he's so hungry. And you come in the night and steal food that should go to them . . . to the children!

MRS. VAN DAAN, *going to Mr. van Daan protectively*.   He needs more food than the rest of us. He's used to more. He's a big man.

Mr. van Daan breaks away, going over and sitting on the couch.

MRS. FRANK, *turning on Mrs. van Daan*.   And you . . . you're worse than he is! You're a mother, and yet you sacrifice your child to this man . . . this . . . this . . .

MR. FRANK.   Edith! Edith!

Margot picks up the pink woollen stole, putting it over her mother's shoulders.

MRS. FRANK, *paying no attention, going on to Mrs. van Daan*. Don't think I haven't seen you! Always saving the choicest bits for him! I've watched you day after day and I've held my tongue. But not any longer! Not after this! Now I want him to go! I want him to get out of here!

MR. FRANK.   Edith!   } *Together*
MR. VAN DAAN.   Get out of here? }

MRS. VAN DAAN.   What do you mean?

MRS. FRANK.   Just that! Take your things and get out!

MR. FRANK, *to Mrs. Frank*.   You're speaking in anger. You cannot mean what you are saying.

MRS. FRANK.   I mean exactly that!

Mrs. van Daan takes a cover from the Franks' bed, pulling it about her.

MR. FRANK.   For two long years we have lived here, side by side. We have respected each other's rights . . . we have managed to live in peace. Are we now going to throw it all away?

I know this will never happen again, will it, Mr. van Daan?

MR. VAN DAAN. No. No.

MRS. FRANK. He steals once! He'll steal again!

Mr. van Daan, holding his stomach, starts for the bathroom. Anne puts her arms around him, helping him up the step.

MR. FRANK. Edith, please. Let us be calm. We'll all go to our rooms . . . and afterwards we'll sit down quietly and talk this out . . . we'll find some way . . .

MRS. FRANK. No! No! No more talk! I want them to leave!

MRS. VAN DAAN. You'd put us out, on the streets?

MRS. FRANK. There are other hiding places.

MRS. VAN DAAN. A cellar . . . a closet. I know. And we have no money left even to pay for that.

MRS. FRANK. I'll give you money. Out of my own pocket I'll give it gladly.

She gets her purse from a shelf and comes back with it.

MRS. VAN DAAN. Mr. Frank, you told Putti you'd never forget what he'd done for you when you came to Amsterdam. You said you could never repay him, that you . . .

MRS. FRANK, *counting out money*. If my husband had any obligation to you, he's paid it, over and over.

MR. FRANK. Edith, I've never seen you like this before. I don't know you.

MRS. FRANK. I should have spoken out long ago.

DUSSEL. You can't be nice to some people.

MRS. VAN DAAN, *turning on Dussel*. There would have been plenty for all of us, if *you* hadn't come in here!

MR. FRANK. We don't need the Nazis to destroy us. We're destroying ourselves.

He sits down, with his head in his hands. Mrs. Frank goes to Mrs. van Daan.

MRS. FRANK, *giving Mrs. van Daan some money*. Give this to Miep. She'll find you a place.

ANNE. Mother, you're not putting *Peter* out. Peter hasn't done anything.

MRS. FRANK.   He'll stay, of course. When I say I must protect the children, I mean Peter too.

Peter rises from the steps where he has been sitting.

PETER.   I'd have to go if Father goes.

Mr. van Daan comes from the bathroom. Mrs. van Daan hurries to him and takes him to the couch. Then she gets water from the sink to bathe his face.

MRS. FRANK, *while this is going on.*   He's no father to you . . . that man! He doesn't know what it is to be a father!

PETER, *starting for his room.*   I wouldn't feel right. I couldn't stay.

MRS. FRANK.   Very well, then. I'm sorry.

ANNE, *rushing over to Peter.*   No, Peter! No! *Peter goes into his room, closing the door after him. Anne turns back to her mother, crying.* I don't care about the food. They can have mine! I don't want it! Only don't send them away. It'll be daylight soon. They'll be caught . . .

MARGOT, *putting her arms comfortingly around Anne.*   Please, Mother!

MRS. FRANK.   They're not going now. They'll stay here until Miep finds them a place. *To Mrs. van Daan.* But one thing I insist on! He must never come down here again! He must never come to this room where the food is stored! We'll divide what we have . . . an equal share for each! *Dussel hurries over to get a sack of potatoes from the food safe. Mrs. Frank goes on, to Mrs. van Daan.* You can cook it here and take it up to him.

Dussel brings the sack of potatoes back to the centre table.

MARGOT.   Oh, no. No. We haven't sunk so far that we're going to fight over a handful of rotten potatoes.

DUSSEL, *dividing the potatoes into piles.*   Mrs. Frank, Mr. Frank, Margot, Anne, Peter, Mrs. van Daan, Mr. van Daan, myself . . . Mrs. Frank . . .

The buzzer sounds in Miep's signal.

MR. FRANK.   It's Miep.

He hurries over, getting his overcoat and putting it on.

MARGOT.   At this hour?

MRS. FRANK.   It is trouble.

MR. FRANK, *as he starts down to unbolt the door.*   I beg you, don't let her see a thing like this!

MR. DUSSEL, *counting without stopping.*   . . . Anne, Peter, Mrs. van Daan, Mr. van Daan, myself . . .

MARGOT, *to Dussel.*   Stop it! Stop it!

DUSSEL.   . . . Mr. Frank, Margot, Anne, Peter, Mrs. van Daan, Mr. van Daan, myself, Mrs. Frank . . .

MRS. VAN DAAN.   You're keeping the big ones for yourself! All the big ones . . . Look at the size of that! . . . And that! . . .

Dussel continues with his dividing. Peter, with his shirt and trousers on, comes from his room.

MARGOT.   Stop it! Stop it!

We hear Miep's excited voice speaking to Mr. Frank below.

MIEP.   Mr. Frank . . . the most wonderful news! . . . The invasion has begun!

MR. FRANK.   Go on, tell them! Tell them!

Miep comes running up the steps, ahead of Mr. Frank. She has a man's raincoat on over her nightclothes and a bunch of orange-coloured flowers in her hand.

MIEP.   Did you hear that, everybody? Did you hear what I said? The invasion has begun! The invasion!

They all stare at Miep, unable to grasp what she is telling them. Peter is the first to recover his wits.

PETER.   Where?

MRS. VAN DAAN.   When? When, Miep?

MIEP.   It began early this morning . . .

As she talks on, the realization of what she has said begins to dawn on them. Everyone goes crazy. A wild demonstration takes place. Mrs. Frank hugs Mr. van Daan.

MRS. FRANK.   Oh, Mr. van Daan, did you hear that?

Dussel embraces Mrs. van Daan. Peter grabs a frying pan and parades around the room, beating on it, singing the Dutch National Anthem. Anne and Margot follow him, singing, weaving in and out among the excited grownups. Margot breaks away to take the flowers from Miep and distribute them to everyone. While this pandemonium is going on Mrs. Frank tries to make herself heard above the excitement.

MRS. FRANK, *to Miep.* How do you know?

MIEP. The radio . . . The B.B.C.! They said they landed on the coast of Normandy!

PETER. The British?

MIEP. British, Americans, French, Dutch, Poles, Norwegians . . . all of them! More than four thousand ships! Churchill spoke, and General Eisenhower! D-Day they call it!

MR. FRANK. Thank God, it's come!

MRS. VAN DAAN. At last!

MIEP, *starting out.* I'm going to tell Mr. Kraler. This'll be better than any blood transfusion.

MR. FRANK, *stopping her.* What part of Normandy did they land, did they say?

MIEP. Normandy . . . that's all I know now . . . I'll be up the minute I hear some more!

She goes hurriedly out.

MR. FRANK, *to Mrs. Frank.* What did I tell you? What did I tell you?

Mrs. Frank indicates that he has forgotten to bolt the door after Miep. He hurries down the steps. Mr. van Daan, sitting on the couch, suddenly breaks into a convulsive sob. Everybody looks at him, bewildered.

MRS. VAN DAAN, *hurrying to him.* Putti! Putti! What is it? What happened?

MR. VAN DAAN. Please. I'm so ashamed.

Mr. Frank comes back up the steps.

DUSSEL. Oh, for God's sake!

MRS. VAN DAAN. Don't, Putti.

◄——— **The invasion has begun!**

MARGOT.   It doesn't matter now!

MR. FRANK, *going to Mr. van Daan.*   Didn't you hear what Miep said? The invasion has come! We're going to be liberated! This is a time to celebrate!

He embraces Mrs. Frank and then hurries to the cupboard and gets the cognac and a glass.

MR. VAN DAAN.   To steal bread from children!

MRS. FRANK.   We've all done things that we're ashamed of.

ANNE.   Look at me, the way I've treated Mother . . . so mean and horrid to her.

MRS. FRANK.   No, Anneke, no.

Anne runs to her mother, putting her arms around her.

ANNE.   Oh, Mother, I was. I was awful.

MR. VAN DAAN.   Not like me. No one is as bad as me!

DUSSEL, *to Mr. van Daan.*   Stop it now! Let's be happy!

MR. FRANK, *giving Mr. van Daan a glass of cognac.*   Here! Here! *Schnapps! Locheim!*

Van Daan takes the cognac. They all watch him. He gives them a feeble smile. Anne puts up her fingers in a V-for-Victory sign. As van Daan gives an answering V-sign, they are startled to hear a loud sob from behind them. It is Mrs. Frank, stricken with remorse. She is sitting on the other side of the room.

MRS. FRANK, *through her sobs.*   When I think of the terrible things I said . . .

Mr. Frank, Anne and Margot hurry to her, trying to comfort her. Mr. van Daan brings her his glass of cognac.

MR. VAN DAAN.   No! No! You were right!

MRS. FRANK.   That I should speak that way to you! . . . Our friends! . . . Our guests!

She starts to cry again.

DUSSEL.   Stop it, you're spoiling the whole invasion!

As they are comforting her, the lights dim out. The curtain falls.

ANNE'S VOICE, *faintly at first and then with growing strength.* We're all in much better spirits these days. There's still excellent news of the invasion. The best part about it is that I have a feeling that friends are coming. Who knows? Maybe I'll be back in school by fall. Ha, ha! The joke is on us! The warehouse man doesn't know a thing and we are paying him all that money! .. Wednesday, the second of July, nineteen forty-four. The invasion seems temporarily to be bogged down. Mr. Kraler has to have an operation, which looks bad. The Gestapo have found the radio that was stolen. Mr. Dussel says they'll trace it back and back to the thief, and then, it's just a matter of time till they get to us. Everyone is low. Even poor Pim can't raise their spirits. I have often been downcast myself . . . but never in despair. I can shake off everything if I write. But . . . and that is the great question . . . will I ever be able to write well? I want to so much. I want to go on living even after my death. Another birthday has gone by, so now I am fifteen. Already I know what I want. I have a goal, an opinion.

As this is being said—the curtain rises on the scene, the lights dim on, and Anne's voice fades out.

SCENE 4

It is an afternoon a few weeks later . . . Everyone but Margot is in the main room. There is a sense of great tension.

Both Mrs. Frank and Mr. van Daan are nervously pacing back and forth, Dussel is standing at the window, looking down fixedly at the street below. Peter is at the centre table, trying to do his lessons. Anne sits opposite him, writing in her diary. Mrs. van Daan is seated on the couch, her eyes on Mr. Frank as he sits reading.

The sound of a telephone ringing comes from the office below. They all are rigid, listening tensely. Mr. Dussel rushes down to Mr. Frank.

DUSSEL. There it goes again, the telephone! Mr. Frank, do you hear?

MR. FRANK, *quietly*.   Yes. I hear.

DUSSEL, *pleading, insistent*.   But this is the third time, Mr. Frank! The third time in quick succession! It's a signal! I tell you it's Miep, trying to get us! For some reason she can't come to us and she's trying to warn us of something!

MR. FRANK.   Please. Please.

MR. VAN DAAN, *to Dussel*.   You're wasting your breath.

DUSSEL.   Something has happened, Mr. Frank. For three days now Miep hasn't been to see us! And today not a man has come to work. There hasn't been a sound in the building!

MRS. FRANK.   Perhaps it's Sunday.   We may have lost track of the days.

MR. VAN DAAN, *to Anne*.   You with the diary there. What day is it?

DUSSEL, *going to Mrs. Frank*.   I don't lose track of the days! I know exactly what day it is! It's Friday, the fourth of August. Friday, and not a man at work. *He rushes back to Mr. Frank, pleading with him, almost in tears*. I tell you Mr. Kraler's dead. That's the only explanation. He's dead and they've closed down the building, and Miep's trying to tell us!

MR. FRANK.   She'd never telephone us.

DUSSEL, *frantic*.   Mr. Frank, answer that! I beg you, answer it!

MR FRANK.   No.

MR. VAN DAAN.   Just pick it up and listen. You don't have to speak. Just listen and see if it's Miep.

DUSSEL, *speaking at the same time*.   For God's sake . . . I ask you.

MR. FRANK.   No. I've told you, no. I'll do nothing that might let anyone know we're in the building.

PETER.   Mr. Frank's right.

MR. VAN DAAN.   There's no need to tell us what side you're on.

MR. FRANK.   If we wait patiently, quietly, I believe that help will come.

There is silence for a minute as they all listen to the telephone ringing.

DUSSEL. I'm going down. *He rushes down the steps. Mr. Frank tries ineffectually to hold him. Dussel runs to the lower door, unbolting it. The telephone stops ringing. Dussel bolts the door and comes slowly back up the steps.* Too late. *Mr. Frank goes to Margot in Anne's bedroom.*

MR. VAN DAAN. So we just wait here until we die.

MRS. VAN DAAN, *hysterically.* I can't stand it! I'll kill myself! I'll kill myself!

MR. VAN DAAN. For God's sake, stop it!

In the distance, a German military band is heard playing a Viennese waltz.

MRS. VAN DAAN. I think you'd be glad if I did! I think you want me to die!

MR. VAN DAAN. Whose fault is it we're here? *Mrs. van Daan starts for her room. He follows, talking at her.* We could've been safe somewhere . . . in America or Switzerland. But no! No! You wouldn't leave when I wanted to. You couldn't leave your things. You couldn't leave your precious furniture.

MRS. VAN DAAN. Don't touch me!

She hurries up the stairs, followed by Mr. van Daan. Peter, unable to bear it, goes to his room. Anne looks after him, deeply concerned. Dussel returns to his post at the window. Mr. Frank comes back into the main room and takes a book, trying to read. Mrs. Frank sits near the sink, starting to peel some potatoes. Anne quietly goes to Peter's room, closing the door after her. Peter is lying face down on the cot. Anne leans over him, holding him in her arms, trying to bring him out of his despair.

ANNE. Look, Peter, the sky. *She looks up through the skylight.* What a lovely, lovely day! Aren't the clouds beautiful? You know what I do when it seems as if I couldn't stand being cooped up for one more minute? I *think* myself out. I think myself on a walk in the park where I used to go with Pim. Where the jonquils and the crocus and the violets grow down the slopes. You know the most wonderful part about *thinking* yourself out? You can have it any way you like. You can have roses and violets and chrysanthemums all blooming at the same time . . . It's funny . . . I used to take it all for granted . . . and now I've gone crazy about everything to do with nature. Haven't you?

PETER. I've just gone crazy. I think if something doesn't happen soon . . . if we don't get out of here . . . I can't stand much more of it!

ANNE, *softly*. I wish you had a religion, Peter.

PETER. No, thanks! Not me!

ANNE. Oh, I don't mean you have to be Orthodox . . . or believe in heaven and hell and purgatory and things . . . I just mean some religion . . . it doesn't matter what. Just to believe in something! When I think of all that's out there . . . the trees . . . and flowers . . . and seagulls . . . when I think of the dearness of you, Peter . . . and the goodness of the people we know . . . Mr. Kraler, Miep, Dirk, the vegetable man, all risking their lives for us every day . . . When I think of these good things, I'm not afraid any more . . . I find myself, and God, and I . . .

Peter interrupts, getting up and walking away.

PETER. That's fine! But when I begin to think, I get mad! Look at us, hiding out for two years. Not able to move! Caught here like . . . waiting for them to come and get us . . . and all for what?

ANNE. We're not the only people that've had to suffer. There've always been people that've had to . . . sometimes one race . . . sometimes another . . . and yet . . .

PETER. That doesn't make me feel any better!

ANNE, *going to him*. I know it's terrible, trying to have any faith . . . when people are doing such horrible . . . But you know what I sometimes think? I think the world may be going through a phase, the way I was with Mother. It'll pass, maybe not for hundreds of years, but some day . . . I still believe, in spite of everything, that people are really good at heart.

PETER. I want to see something now . . . Not a thousand years from now!

He goes over, sitting down again on the cot.

ANNE. But, Peter, if you'd only look at it as part of a great pattern . . . that we're just a little minute in the life . . . *She breaks off.* Listen to us, going at each other like a couple of stupid grownups! Look at the sky now. Isn't it lovely? *She holds out her hand to him. Peter takes it and rises, standing with her at the window looking out, his arms around her.* Some day, when we're outside again, I'm going to . . .

She breaks off as she hears the sound of a car, its brakes squealing as it comes to a sudden stop. The people in the other rooms also become aware of the sound. They listen tensely. Another car roars up to a screeching stop. Anne and Peter come from Peter's room. Mr. and Mrs. van Daan creep down the stairs. Dussel comes out from his room. Everyone is listening, hardly breathing. A doorbell clangs again and again in the building below. Mr. Frank starts quietly down the steps to the door. Dussel and Peter follow him. The others stand rigid, waiting, terrified.

In a few seconds Dussel comes stumbling back up the steps. He shakes off Peter's help and goes to his room. Mr. Frank bolts the door below, and comes slowly back up the steps. Their eyes are all on him as he stands there for a minute. They realize that what they feared has happened. Mrs. van Daan starts to whimper. Mr. van Daan puts her gently in a chair, and then hurries off up the stairs to their room to collect their things. Peter goes to comfort his mother. There is a sound of violent pounding on a door below.

MR. FRANK, *quietly.* For the past two years we have lived in fear. Now we can live in hope.

The pounding below becomes more insistent. There are muffled sounds of voices, shouting commands.

MEN'S VOICES. *Auf machen! Da drinnen! Auf machen! Schnell! Schnell! Schnell! etc., etc.*

The street door below is forced open. We hear the heavy tread of footsteps coming up. Mr. Frank gets two school bags from the shelves, and gives one to Anne and the other to Margot. He goes to get a bag for Mrs. Frank. The sound of feet coming up grows louder. Peter comes to Anne, kissing her good-bye, then he goes to his room to collect his things. The buzzer of their door starts to ring. Mr. Frank brings Mrs. Frank a bag. They stand together, waiting. We hear the thud of gun butts on the door, trying to break it down.

Anne stands, holding her school satchel, looking over at her father and mother with a soft, reassuring smile. She is no longer a child, but a woman with courage to meet whatever lies ahead.

The lights dim out. The curtain falls on the scene. We hear a mighty crash as the door is shattered. After a second Anne's voice is heard.

ANNE'S VOICE.   And so it seems our stay here is over. They are waiting for us now. They've allowed us five minutes to get our things. We can each take a bag and whatever it will hold of clothing. Nothing else. So, dear Diary, that means I must leave you behind. Good-bye for a while. P.S. Please, please, Miep, or Mr. Kraler, or anyone else. If you should find this diary, will you please keep it safe for me, because some day I hope . . .

Her voice stops abruptly. There is silence. After a second the curtain rises.

SCENE 5

It is again the afternoon in November, 1945. The rooms are as we saw them in the first scene. Mr. Kraler has joined Miep and Mr. Frank. There are coffee cups on the table. We see a great change in Mr. Frank. He is calm now. His bitterness is gone. He slowly turns a few pages of the diary. They are blank.

MR. FRANK.   No more.

He closes the diary and puts it down on the couch beside him.

MIEP.   I'd gone to the country to find food. When I got back the block was surrounded by police . . .

MR. KRALER.   We made it our business to learn how they knew. It was the thief . . . the thief who told them.

Miep goes up to the gas burner, bringing back a pot of coffee.

MR. FRANK, *after a pause.*   It seems strange to say this, that anyone could be happy in a concentration camp. But Anne was happy in the camp in Holland where they first took us.

After two years of being shut up in these rooms, she could be out . . . out in the sunshine and the fresh air that she loved.

MIEP, *offering the coffee to Mr. Frank.* A little more?

MR. FRANK, *holding out his cup to her.* The news of the war was good. The British and Americans were sweeping through France. We felt sure that they would get to us in time. In September we were told that we were to be shipped to Poland . . . The men to one camp. The women to another. I was sent to Auschwitz. They went to Belsen. In January we were freed, the few of us who were left. The war wasn't yet over, so it took us a long time to get home. We'd be sent here and there behind the lines where we'd be safe. Each time our train would stop . . . at a siding, or a crossing . . . we'd all get out and go from group to group . . . Where were you? Were you at Belsen? At Buchenwald? At Mauthausen? Is it possible that you knew my wife? Did you ever see my husband? My son? My daughter? That's how I found out about my wife's death . . . of Margot, the van Daans . . . Dussel. But Anne . . . I still hoped . . . Yesterday I went to Rotterdam. I'd heard of a woman there . . . She'd been in Belsen with Anne . . . I know now.

He picks up the diary again, and turns the pages back to find a certain passage. As he finds it we hear Anne's voice.

ANNE'S VOICE. In spite of everything, I still believe that people are really good at heart.

Mr. Frank slowly closes the diary.

MR. FRANK. She puts me to shame.

They are silent.

The Curtain Falls.

HISTORICAL BACKGROUND

In the elections of March 1933, the National Socialist German Workers' party (the Nazi party) gained a majority, and Adolph Hitler, the man who had emerged as its leader, was called upon to form a government. The party's official programme—nationalism, rearmament, aggression, and racism—was now re-defined and certain of its aspects given greater emphasis in the first 4-year plan.

An important Nazi doctrine was race purity. This was derived from a belief set forth by certain pseudo-scientific writers of the nineteenth century to the effect that, since some races of the world are superior to others, the most excellent society must be that composed exclusively of members of the highest race; the highest race is the Aryan race, to which the Germans belong. (It need hardly be said that this belief is unsupported by present conclusions of biology, ethnology, and history.)

Under the Nazis, the doctrine of race purity, and its ultimate aim to build up the best possible state, was a gigantic façade. The campaign for race purity, which necessitated the removal from German society of non-Aryan peoples (in effect, Communists and Jews), functioned under Dr. Goebbels as a high-propaganda tool by means of which the Nazi party was able to strengthen its political position.

The significance of anti-semitism (an important negative aspect of race purity, as interpreted by the Nazis) lay in its appeal for the lower middle classes in Germany, which were suffering from the effects of the great economic depression of the nineteen thirties, which had hit Germany with particular severity. It was not difficult to impregnate the minds of hungry people with a doctrine—shouted by Hitler, himself no mean orator; broadcast from state-controlled radio stations; and printed in mass-circulated newspapers—which promised a new Germany, peopled with supermen (among whom thousands of Germans visualized themselves); a Germany whose prosperity was guaranteed by its official spokesman, *Der Führer,* and whose symbol was the "people's car".

Under the Nazi régime, the position of the Jews in Germany became intolerable. Most of them were city dwellers, and soon found themselves segregated in ghettos, formed by building walls across streets which gave access to Jewish quarters. Their synagogues were burned; their business premises destroyed in terrorist attacks. In 1935, Jews were deprived of German citizenship; in the following year, by law and by force, they were ejected from public employment, in the usual sense, although, at a later date, many Jews were conscripted for slave labour in German war industries.

By 1941, the extermination camps were in operation, and the position of the Jews who remained in Germany was one of extreme danger. At Auschwitz, in Poland, were built large gas chambers in which hundreds of Jews were murdered at one time. Incinerators disposed of the bodies so quickly that, at peak production, a rate of 6,000 executions a day was reached!

It has been said that the life and outlook of the average German citizen who lived near and through this greatest mass-murder of recorded history were virtually unaffected by it. Some of the more thoughtful probably wondered, uneasily, at the smoke belching from Belsen's chimneys; but the train loads of living Jewish freight passed, for the most part, in the night, and the state-controlled radio stations and the mass-circulated newspapers did not carry these horror tales. Or perhaps some people did think and say nothing. Fear is a great silencer of tongues!

The Franks must have considered themselves among the fortunate, when, in 1933, they were safely out of Germany and into Holland. If so, their reprieve was short lived. In 1940, when German troops moved into the Netherlands, all Jews (Dutch-born and refugees) were discriminated against, and, finally, relentlessly hunted down. Of all the countries conquered by Hitler, Holland, which is small in area, flat and treeless (in many parts), and already over-populated, was the one in which it was most difficult for a Jew to hide—and this despite the fact that many Dutch Christians took great risks to keep Jewish families out of Nazi hands.

FROM DIARY TO DRAMATIC PRODUCTION

For years after the initial production of *The Diary of Anne Frank* (New York, 1955), this drama played every night, in some part of the world. Every night audiences were caught up in the harried lives of the refugees, shaken out of their customary complacency, profoundly moved and uplifted by the gallant spirit of Anne Frank herself.

In 1956, the play opened simultaneously in Berlin, Dusseldorf, Dresden, Hamburg, Vienna, and Zurich. Since that time, in Western Germany it has had long runs at more than half of the professional theatres, in each of which capacity audiences watched in complete absorption and left without applause.

To adapt the content of the *Diary* to a dramatic form was not an easy task, but, on the whole, this has been done successfully. By its very nature, a diary consists of private thoughts, revela-. tions, and impressions. When these are converted to dramatic form, not only must they be expressed vocally, but also (in many instances) re-expressed in the terms and idiom of the individual characters of the drama. The sense of confinement, frustration, and helplessness that the occupants of the annex undergo during the hours, days, and years of hiding is admirably conveyed. Like the *Diary*, the play has an unexpected buoyancy; situations, in themselves tense, and terrible in implication, are relieved by flashes of humour and skilful contrasts of mood and event. But when the authors attempt to express the emotion which Anne feels herself experiencing for Peter (an emotion which she herself cannot adequately analyze), the dramatic form appears to be less effective.

The Diary of Anne Frank can be done very successfully by secondary-school dramatic groups. An amateur acting edition with very full stage directions is available. Please see note on page iv.

KEY TO PRONUNCIATIONS

Amen	Oh-mein	Kerli	Care'-lee
Amsterdam	Ahm'-ster-dahm	Kraler	Krah'-ler
Anne	Ah'-nah *or the familiar* Ah'-nee	Liefje	Leaf'-yah
		Margot	Mar'-gott
Anneke	Ah'-nah-kah	Mauthausen	Maut'-how-sen
Anneline	Ah'-nah-lynn	Mazeltov	Mah'-zel-tahv
Auschwitz	Aow'-shvitz	Miep	Meep
Belsen	Bell'-sen	Mouschi	Moo'-she
Buchenwald	Buch'-en-vald	Otto	Ah'-toe
Delphi	Dell'-fie	Peter	Pay'-ter
Dirk	Dee'-urk	Petronella	Pet-row-nell'-ah
Dussel	Duss'-ell	Putti	Poo'-tee
Edith	Ae'-dit	Rotterdam	Rah'-ter-dahm
Frank	Frahnk	Van Daan	Fahn Dahn
Hallensteins	Ha'-len-stains	Wessels	Vess'-ells
Hilversum	Hill'-ver-sum	Westertoren	Vess'-ter-tor-en
Jan	Yan	Wilhelmina	Vil-hel-mee'-nah
Jopie	Yo'-pee		

NOTES AND QUESTIONS

Act One: *Scene 1*

3 **"Monday, the sixth of July":** In fact, the first entry in Anne Frank's diary was made on Sunday, 14 June 1942. There was no entry for Monday, 6 July 1942—the day the Franks went into hiding.

"When Hitler came to power": the year 1933. After the March election, Adolph Hitler, leader of the National Socialist German Workers' party (the Nazi party) was called upon to form a government

"Then things got very bad for the Jews": This refers, of course, to the Nazi-German persecution of Jews throughout Europe in the Second World War. An estimated five million Jews were exterminated during these years, mostly through starvation and direct murder in prison camps. (It should be remembered that many [non-Jewish] Germans who did not belong to the Nazi party risked their lives to give shelter to Jewish families and to assist them to leave the country.)

"We had to wear yellow stars": This is a reference to the Star of David—the six-pointed star, made from yellow-coloured cloth, and symbolic of Judaism. In mediaeval times, Jews were required to wear the Star of David, as a distinguishing badge of their race. The custom was revived by the Nazis.

QUESTIONS

1. At what point in the Frank story does the play open?
2. Describe the general mood or tone of the opening scene. What details have the dramatists selected to create this mood?
3. By what device is Anne Frank brought into the play?
4. What information are we given about Anne in this scene?
5. Describe the conditions under which the Jewish emigrants lived in Holland in 1940.
6. How does the ending of the opening scene create suspense?
7. "The opening scene of a play is always a severe test of the playwright's power. He has (a) to make his characters say what seems natural in the given situation, (b) to supply the audience (through the conversation of the characters) with all the information needed to follow the story, and (c) to capture the interest of the audience at the earliest possible moment." Discuss to what extent in the opening scene of *The Diary of Anne Frank* the playwrights accomplish these aims.

91

Act One: *Scene 2*

4 **"plus fours"**: long, wide knickers; so-called because, to produce
an overhang, the length was increased by four inches; usually
worn with knee-length stockings

5 **Green Police** (*Grüne Polizei*): a branch of the Gestapo, or
secret state police force, which was actively employed in appre-
hending Jews in Occupied Holland; so-called from the colour
of their uniforms

mercurial: quick-moving (a quality possessed by the metal,
mercury) ; in this context, subject to quick changes of mood

ration books: small booklets, issued to Dutch citizens in war-
time, and containing coupons for the purchase of limited sup-
plies of food and clothing. The purpose of ration books was to
prevent hoarding, and thus effect a fair distribution of available
goods. During the Second World War, ration books were issued
by the Canadian Government for the same reasons.

6 **black market:** the illegal selling of goods, especially in violation
of rationing or price control regulations

Westertoren: The bell tower of the Westerkerk (1631), a church
situated in the old part of the city of Amsterdam

7 **w.c.:** water closet, or lavatory

9 **fixed:** neutered

11 **my movie stars:** The Secret Annex, or *achterhuis*, of 263 Prin-
sengracht, in Amsterdam, attracts thousands of visitors from all
over the world each year. On the walls of Anne Frank's small
room are post-card photos of film stars Ginger Rogers, Ray
Milland, Deanna Durbin, and Sonja Henie.

Queen Wilhelmina: Queen of the Netherlands from 1890-1948;
during the Nazi occupation she was forced to seek refuge in
England, where she was active in the Dutch resistance movement to German oppression. Like the movie stars, Queen Wilhelmina was one of the "pin-ups" in Anne Frank's room.

14 **Nazis:** refers to the National Socialist German Workers' party;
from 1933 until it was dissolved at the 3-power conference,
Potsdam, in 1945, the only legal political party in Germany.
Anne Frank is really referring here to the Gestapo, or Nazi
secret state police.

QUESTIONS

1. By what means is Scene II given an effective opening?
2. In what capacities did Mr. Kraler and Miep serve the Franks
and van Daans?

3. What regulations were in effect in the annex (or attic) during the day?

4. Describe your first impression of Anne Frank. By what devices is she made to "come alive"?

5. (a) Mr. Frank is admirably suited to be the leader of the group. Show how his intelligence and optimism help Anne to accept new and difficult conditions.
(b) What other qualities does Mr. Frank show in his relationships with Kraler, Miep, and the van Daans?

6. In addition to telling us general news, Anne's diary is an intimate account of her own life as a maturing personality. How is this fact made clear in her off-stage speech at the end of Scene II?

7. (a) How do the actions and personality of Mr. Frank (in Scene II) contrast with his actions and personality in Scene I?
(b) In what way does this contrast increase the dramatic impact of the opening of Scene II?

8. When Anne and Peter are left alone in the living-room (pp. 10-11), what contrasts between them can you deduce from their conversation?

9. For what reason does Mr. Frank interrupt this conversation?

Act One: *Scene 3*

17 **Mazeltov:** a Yiddish word for the Hebrew *mazel* (luck) and *tov* (good)—good luck; clearly, in this instance, a non-commital response

18 **Quack! Quack!:** The incident of the composition assignment, imposed on Anne for chattering, is recounted in the *Diary*, under the date of 12th June, 1942, where it is given a slightly different emphasis.

24 *liefje:* dear (Dutch)

26 **"Every time I hear that sound, my heart stops!":** The buzzer signal used by Miep and Mr. Kraler was the International Code —"V". The British Broadcasting Corporation used it first as a signal to attract listeners in Occupied Europe. Afterward, Churchill adopted the V-sign as a symbol of victory. It is not difficult to understand its appropriateness for the occupants of the annex.

QUESTIONS

1. "So what? And you're sixteen. Just perfect. Your father's ten years older than I am." (page 17) What does Mrs. van Daan reveal of herself when she makes this remark?

2. Point out examples of humour in Scene III.

3. What effect does the "bickering" between Mr. and Mrs. van Daan have on the atmosphere of the annex?

4. In this Scene, what characteristics of herself does Anne reveal through her speech and actions?

5. (a) Why does Mr. van Daan suggest (to his wife) that she be more guarded in her remarks in the presence and hearing of Anne?
   (b) Explain the humour inherent in his suggestion.

6. In what ways does the coming of Mr. Dussel complicate life in the annex?

7. How are the character and personality of (i) Anne, (ii) Mrs. Frank, (iii) Mr. Frank, and (iv) the three van Daans revealed by their various reactions to Dussel's arrival?

8. Although they have only been in the annex for two months, the refugees are already showing the strain of close confinement. Give three instances to support this statement.

9. What dramatic purposes are served by the presentation of Anne's voice at the close of this scene?

Act One: *Scene 4*

34 **"Lili Marlene":** The lyric of this song was written by the German poet, Hans Leip, in 1923. It was set to music by Norbert Schultze, in 1938. By altering the "beat", "Lili Marlene" was converted into a marching song and was very popular with the Nazi troops in the Second World War. When the Nazis took over the Belgrade radio station in 1941, they found there only three records, of which "Lili Marlene" was one. Hence it was played twice nightly. British soldiers stationed in Tobruk, North Africa, became familiar with the song from this recording, and it became very popular with them, as well.

QUESTIONS

1. How is the opening of Scene IV made effective?

2. (a) Describe some of the problems Anne faces as a young girl.
   (b) To what extent are these problems intensified by the un-natural life she is forced to lead?

3. Define the term "pathos". Select three examples of pathos from Scene IV.

4. Show, with reference to the text, how the dramatists use humour to lighten the mood of this scene.

Act One: *Scene 5*

39 **Hanukkah:** Jewish festival commemorating the re-dedication of the Temple by Judas Maccabeus in 165 B.C.; popularly called the "Festival of the Lights", and held in December

40 **"Like our St. Nicholas' Day":** Mr. Dussel makes a "point" of being Dutch. St. Nicholas' Day is celebrated in Holland on

December the sixth, with much the same merriment that most
Canadians celebrate Christmas Day. In Holland, Christmas Day
is observed as a holy day.
latkes: potato pancakes

QUESTIONS

1. In what way is Mrs. Frank's opening prayer appropriate to the
situation in which the families are now living?
2. What qualities does Anne reveal in the incident of the Hanukkah
presents?
3. How is an atmosphere of suspense developed in this scene?
4. "Mr. Frank plays the role of leader admirably in this crisis."
Explain.
5. How do the atmosphere and events of the first part of this scene
heighten the dramatic effect of the sudden noise in the warehouse?
6. Suggest reasons why the singing of the Hanukkah song at the
end of the scene is appropriate.

Act Two: *Scene 1*

64 **Toscanini:** Italian composer, cellist, and musical conductor; in
1898, was appointed chief conductor and artistic director at La
Scala, Milan; appeared as conductor with many famous or-
chestras in Europe and North America. Toscanini was con-
sistently anti-fascist, and several times refused to conduct in
fascist-dominated countries. He made no public appearances as
a musician after 1954, and died in 1957.
"Ride of the Valkyries": the Overture to Richard Wagner's
opera *"Die Walküre"*, composed in 1854-6

QUESTIONS

1. (a) How does the gift of the cake create tension in the annex?
(b) What does it reveal about the characters of Mr. and Mrs.
van Daan?
2. State, in a few words, your opinion of Mr. van Daan in the
matter of the fur-coat episode of this scene.
3. How does the (possible) blackmailer further complicate an already tense situation in the annex?
4. "It isn't our fault that the world is in such a mess! We weren't
around when all this started." (page 61) Comment on the truth
of Anne's statement.
5. Explain how the relationship between Peter and Anne is gradually developing.
6. This scene ends on a note of great tension—a tension which has

been accumulating throughout the scene. From the text, select details which substantiate this statement.

Act Two: *Scene 2*

72 **La Belle Nivernaise:** a delightful story, written in 1886 by Alphonse Daudet (1840-97); a popular choice for extensive reading in the senior grades of secondary schools in Canada. Thus, compared to the average English-speaking Canadian student, Anne was advanced in her reading of French. An entry in the *Diary* for the 8th of May 1944 states: "I'd adore to go to Paris for a year and London for a year and learn the languages. . . ."

QUESTIONS

1. Contrast the attitudes of Mrs. van Daan and Mrs. Frank to the growing friendship between Peter and Anne.
2. Select details of their conversation which show that Peter and Anne are typical young people encountering normal problems as they gradually mature.
3. Why are such simple meetings, as the one described in this scene, of special importance to Peter and Anne?
4. A theatre critic has stated: "Scenes such as this between Peter and Anne are too full of sentimentality and thus falsify the portrait of Anne." With reference to the text of the play, defend (or refute) this opinion.

Act Two: *Scene 3*

79 **B.B.C.:** The British Broadcasting Corporation, London (England). During the Second World War, it performed an important service by broadcasting to people in Nazi-occupied parts of Europe information about the progress of the Allied forces.

Churchill: Sir Winston Churchill (1874—), British statesman, soldier, and author; became Prime Minister of Great Britain in 1940. His energy, stirring oratory, and stubborn refusal to make peace with Hitler were crucial points in maintaining the Allies' resistance to Germany from 1940-42.

General Eisenhower: Dwight David Eisenhower (1890—); United States general commanding the Allied forces in Europe against Nazi Germany; afterward, 34th president of the United States

D-Day: the 6th of June 1944; The "D" is an abbreviation for *day*—repetition for the sake of emphasis. "D-Day" and "H-Hour" were expressions first used in an Order of the United States army on the 7th of Sept. 1918, for the attack on the St. Mihiel area of France.

80 **Schnapps:** literally, strong Holland gin; used here with the
   force of the Norwegian *Skol!* or the English, "Here's looking at
   you!"

   Locheim!: a variant of l'chaim (literally, "To life")—an He-
   braic toast

81 **Gestapo:** German Secret State Police (GEheime STAats POlizei)

QUESTIONS

1. "The incident of the stolen bread is an illustration of a basic
   defect in Mr. van Daan's character." In a short paragraph, and
   with reference to the text, defend or refute this statement.

2. Contrast the emotional state of the characters immediately before
   and immediately after they received the news of the Allied invasion of Western Europe.

3. "From the present-day reader's point of view, Anne Frank's excitement about the success of the invasion is both ironic and
   pathetic." Discuss in a short paragraph.

4. In what way are Mr. Dussell's remarks about the stolen radio a
   foreshadowing of events to come?

5. Why does Anne Frank regard writing as a necessity?

6. "I want to go on living even after my death." In what way do you
   consider Anne Frank's wish for immortality may have been re-
   alized?

Act Two: *Scene 4*

84 **Orthodox:** In the Western world, Judaism split into three
   branches—Orthodox, Reform, and Conservative. All three
   branches evolved in Germany. In general, Orthodox Judaism
   opposes innovation and adheres to the written law (as set forth
   in the Scriptures) and to the oral, or Talmudic law. (Reform
   Judaism demonstrates a complete serverance from Talmudic
   restrictions; Conservative Judaism admits a continuously evolv-
   ing religious culture, which can absorb foreign influences and
   yet maintain its distinctive culture elements.)

   purgatory: a state or place of temporary punishment, expiation,
   or remorse. This is a Roman Catholic concept, and indicates that
   the Franks were not particularly observant of Jewish religious
   processes.

85 **Auf machen:** Open up!
   Da drinnen!: You in there!
   Schnell! Schnell! Schnell!: Quick! Quick! Quick!
   Note that these commands are spoken in German, not in Dutch.
   Of what is this significant?

QUESTIONS

1. "As this scene opens, the van Daans have reached an emotional breaking point." Discuss.
2. By what ways has Anne attempted to surmount the restrictions of life in the annex?
3. In what terms does Anne visualize the persecution of her race?
4. "I still believe in spite of everything that people are really good at heart." What closing impression of Anne does this statement leave?
5. Define the term "dramatic irony". Give an example of dramatic irony from this scene.

Act II: *Scene 5*

87 **Auschwitz, Belsen, Buchenwald, Mathausen:** notorious Nazi concentration camps in which millions of Jews and oppressed people of other races and religions perished in the Second World War

A recent article by Hans Beynon (*London Observer Service*) states: "The Frank family was held at an Amsterdam police station for several days before being taken to the special camp for Dutch Jews at Westerbork. During the train ride to Westerbork, Anne stared out of the window, so as not to miss any of the countryside flashing by. After three weeks at Westerbork, Auschwitz was the next stop. Here Mrs. Frank died of typhus. After Auschwitz, came, for Margot and Anne, the final destination—Bergen-Belsen. In this camp, Margot Frank fell from her bunk and died quietly. Although Anne's gallant spirit endured to the end, she died, exhausted and emaciated, late in February or early March, 1945. Of the eight persons who hid in the annex, only one is now alive—Anne's father, who lives in Switzerland."

QUESTIONS

1. Explain how the eight occupants of the annex were finally discovered.
2. What is the dramatic purpose in having Anne Frank speak in this scene?
3. Discuss the suitability of Scene V as a conclusion to the play.

GENERAL QUESTIONS

1. Describe the conditions under which the Franks, van Daans, and Mr. Dussel lived for more than two years in the annex.

2. (a) Define the literary terms: suspense, surprise, pathos, conflict, satire, humour.
   (b) Indicate sections of the play in which these devices have been effectively employed.

3. "In every scene, the audience is caught up in a poignant, intensely dramatic situation." Defend this statement by referring to three scenes which have appealed to you in the drama.

4. Show, by specific reference to the text, that this drama keeps the reader's interest at a high level by reason of its constantly changing emotional appeals.

5. "*The Diary of Anne Frank* is a clever mixture of seriousness and comedy." Discuss this statement with reference to specific parts of the text.

6. Discuss the effectiveness of the ending of each act of the play.

7. What purposes are served by the device of having Anne speak between each scene?

8. Of the stage adaptation of Anne's *Diary*, Mr. Frank said: "It is not a play. It is a mission". Explain.

9. The drama critic of a Berlin newspaper wrote: "When, after three hours, as if awakening from deepest embarrassment, the people in the stalls can hardly rise from their seats, will not permit applause, and leave silently and with bowed heads, that marks the greatness of a moment which must rouse the slowest hearts and which must shake the most indifferent nerves." What thoughts and emotions do you suppose were being experienced by these audiences?

10. "*The Diary of Anne Frank* is likely to enjoy a permanent popularity." Defend or refute this statement.

11. Conflict is essential to drama. Discuss three examples of conflict in this play.

12. A dramatist may describe and explain a character to his audience by contrasting that character with others in the play. Show how contrasts help to clarify the characters of (a) Anne Frank; (b) Mr. Frank.

13. "Apart from Anne, the characters in this drama are 'stock' and one-dimensional. They could easily become tiresome." Defend or refute, with reference to the text.

14. Throughout the drama, all the occupants of the annex know they are in imminent danger of extermination. Yet the van Daans and Mr. Dussel appear to be intent on creating misery.

Discuss, with reference to the play, whether extreme adversity brings out the worst or the best in human nature.

15. In your opinion, was Anne's interest in Peter van Daan engendered mainly by circumstances, and her great need to love (and to be loved) or by a genuine emotion of love? Discuss, with reference to the text.

16. In Act One, Scene III, Mr. Frank states: "We don't need the Nazis to destroy us. We're destroying ourselves." To what extent may Mr. Frank be considered as a symbol of intelligence or reason trying to impose order on chaos?

17. This drama is based on material found in Anne Frank's *Diary*. Giving reasons, state which form (narrative or dramatic) is more effective in presenting Anne's experiences and changing point of view.

18. Compare the character of Anne Frank and that of the heroine of another play or novel you have recently studied.

19. Under the following headings, contrast *The Diary of Anne Frank* with another play you have studied recently: (a) structure (b) development of suspense (c) the use of humour (d) setting (e) irony.

20. Name the speaker and state the significance of each of the following speeches:
    (a) "We have nothing in common. She doesn't understand me."
    (b) "We are all here alive. That is present enough."
    (c) "I think some day he'll be caught and then he'll make a bargain with the Green Police . . . if they'll let him off, he'll tell them where some Jews are hiding."
    (d) "I've just gone crazy. I think if something doesn't happen soon . . . if we don't get out of here . . . I can't stand much more of it!"
    (e) "For the past two years we have lived in fear. Now we can live in hope."
    (f) "There are no walls, there are no bolts, no locks that anyone can put on your mind."

21. There was much talk about the rescue—and yet this was an external act, or would have been had it been effected. Was there not an opportunity for each member of the annex to "save himself" by an inner redémption, a washing clean by experience? By this interpretation of "rescue", which of the occupants had a chance of survival? Discuss, and state reasons for your opinions.

22. (a) You are living in a democracy. Are you aware of racial

discrimination in the society of which you are a part? Give reasons for your answer.

(b) Can racial discrimination be prevented by laws, alone? Give reasons for your opinion.

(c) What is your position (point of view) on racial discrimination?

(d) What steps (public or otherwise) would you be prepared to take to defend your point of view on racial discrimination?

(e) Could the story of the Frank family ever be enacted in Canada? Discuss.

CHARACTER—QUESTIONNAIRES
Interpretations

A.   Below you will find a character-questionnaire on Anne Frank. It is possible to *surmise* many things about Anne, but what we *know* about her is limited to a consideration of what she does and says (and by what other people say about her) in the drama. For this reason, the character-questionnaire is based on quotations drawn from the text.

(a) Complete the questionnaire by writing (in one or two sentences) your interpretation of each quotation. (What significant thing does it tell about Anne?)

(b) Refer to the interpretations, and write an interesting description of Anne Frank.

1. "With all the boys in the world . . . why I had to get locked up with one like you!" (page 18)

2. "We are now in what is known as the 'bean' cycle! . . ." (page 19)

3. "Anne, you got an excellent in your history paper today and very good in Latin." (Mr. Frank, page 20)

4. "It's a wonder that Miep has a life of her own, the way we make her run errands for us." (page 23)

5. "Talk, talk, talk. I never heard such a child." (Mr. van Daan, page 23)

6. "I'm going to be remarkable. I'm going to Paris . . . to study music and art." (page 24)

7. "You are wild, self-willed." (Mrs. Frank, page 25)

8. "I've got to fight things out for myself . . . make something of myself." (page 25)

9. "Why is it that every grownup thinks he knows the way to bring up children. Particularly the grownups that never had any." (Anne, of Mr. Dussel, page 34)

10. "I'm a terrible coward. I'm so disappointed in myself." (page 37)

11. "I can stand off and look at myself doing it and know it's cruel and yet can't stop doing it. Help me." (page 38)

12. "I have a nicer side . . . a sweeter side." (page 38)

13. "What's the good of thinking of misery when you're already miserable? That's stupid." (page 61)

14. "It isn't our fault that the world is in such a mess! We weren't around when all this started!" (page 61)

15. "Nothing can take the place of school and play and friends your own age . . ." (page 63)

16. "Maybe there's nothing to be jealous of. Maybe he doesn't really like me." (page 67)

17. "It's so hard to try to think what to do, when here we are with the whole world falling about our ears." (page 71)

18. "I can shake off everything if I write . . . but will I ever be able to write well? (page 81)

19. "You know the most wonderful part about *thinking* yourself out? You can have it anyway you like." (page 83)

20. "Look, Peter, the sky! . . . I've gone crazy about everything to do with nature." (pages 83 and 84)

21. "I still believe, in spite of everything, that people are really good at heart." (page 84)

B.   (a) Make up a set of quotations for one of the following characters: Mr. Frank, Mrs. Frank, Mr. van Daan, Mrs. van Daan, Peter van Daan, and Margot Frank. (b) Write down the interpretation. (c) Then write an interesting description of the person.

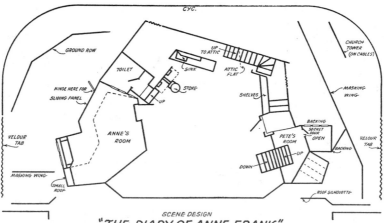

SCENE DESIGN
"*THE DIARY OF ANNE FRANK*"